THE CINEPHILE
CATALOGUE

THE TOTALLY INTERACTIVE MOVIE BOOK FOR MOVIE LOVERS

Volume 4: 1989-Before 1910

ANTONIO POLANCO

Written and Directed
by

_____

First edition - Feb 2023

Book design by Oliva Pro Design
Editing by Michaela Choi

ISBN: 979-8-9866045-0-3 (Paperback), 979-8-9866045-7-2 (eBook)
Library of Congress Control Number: 2022918031

ACKNOWLEDGEMENTS

These generous and extraordinary people
helped make this book a reality
and gave some much-needed hope
when hope was in terribly short supply.

Ben Cook
Darlene Crowder
Anthony Cuni
Henry De La Rosa
Roberto Garcia
William Hauser
Benjamin M. Hutchins
Susan LoVaglio Machado
Alexander Martinez
Camile O'Briant
Douglas Oldiges
Elissa Olin
Karen Otis
Francisco Polanco
Marcy Polanco
Domenico Pontoriero
Yanike Ramirez
Joselyn Rodriguez
Joe Slate
Claire Wasserman

This book is also dedicated to my beautiful familia, whose Love, belief &
support played an essential part in getting this book in your hands…

THE CINEPHILE CATALOGUE - LEGEND

Highest Grossing Film (Worldwide)	Avengers: Endgame
Highest Grossing Film (US)	Finding Dory
Blockbusters & Money Makers (US)	Jaws*
Best Picture - Academy Awards	The Godfather **[2]**
Best Foreign Film - Academy Awards	Cinema Paradiso IT
Best Documentary - Academy Awards (Long & Short)	Searching for Sugar Man
Best Picture - Golden Globes (Drama & Comedy/Musical)	Beauty and the Beast
Best Foreign Film - Golden Globes	Central Station BRZ
Best Documentary - Golden Globes	Elvis on Tour
Criterion Collection	*Mulholland Drive*
Best Film - BAFTA	Dr. Strangelove or: How I Learned to Stop Worrying and Love the Bomb
Palme D'Or - Cannes Film Festival	Pulp Fiction

- Colors correspond to the film winning that category's top prize of Best Film
- Numbers next to films mean it won a major film category but in different award organizations. 2000's "Gladiator" won Best Picture at the Oscars, BAFTA's and the Golden Globes (as Motion Picture Drama), hence the bracketed **[3]** to its right.
- An asterisk (*) next to a film signifies it was a money maker & hit, and blockbuster films with two bold asterisks (**) signify they were nominated for major awards.
- The empty spaces and NOTES sections let you write whatever personal notes, extra marks or comments you want to make. [No rules for your TCC, have fun!!]

Greetings! Peace all around to you and yours!

Welcome to **The Cinephile Catalogue** (or TCC for short). This TCC is meant for *You* dear movie lover, now writer/director. No matter who you are, when you are, how you are, or really why you are… wherever you are on this big beautiful blue rock, this film journal was heartfully, mindfully, and lovingly crafted to turn into a keepsake for years to come!

This custom-built, chronological, cinema catalogue is easy to follow, organized by genres, made to mark and write up however you wish (just like your favorite journal!). Examples of markups can be found on the very next page. There's also ample space between titles and NOTES pages for you. You'll find your movie past, present, and future all coming together. While there are many movies listed here, remember you don't have to do it alone. Feel free to share TCC with a friend, your partner, your family or even your cinema club!

If you're reading this, there's a good chance you watch movies. Who knows, you may have a few favorites! If you're like me, you've seen great movies, so/so movies, and even some awful farkakteh movies. You may make it a point to go out with Dad or Mom, the Mr/Mrs/SO's, kids, friends or whoever out for popcorn and a show. That show is a part of American life and the world at large. Though cinema is relatively new compared to other artforms, movies show us as a people, with all the colors and ways our hearts beat.

Let's quickly flashback to *viente viente*, the year 2020… I tried making the most of the time, as well as I could! Effectively homebound, I caught up on movies, TV series, and documentaries, experiencing stories and cultures I'd never get to see otherwise. Then a simple idea popped in my head, and I started jotting down the best movies of each year into an old journal.

Three years later, a final draft to "The Cinephile Catalogue" was complete. This interactive movie guide was a product of 2020—the perspective, passion, and persistence towards a goal: to finish this darn book… for myself and for every cinephile out there! I'm a lifelong movie lover and getting this book made has been one of the hardest, most fearful, most fulfilling experiences of my Life. I couldn't be happier you now have one in your hands!

On a final note, I sincerely thank You for purchasing this TCC. This book was heavily researched and heartfully crafted for movie lovers by someone who loves movies! With that said, get ready for a once-in-a-lifetime trip through the whole of film history, and a special look back at your movie history. Grab a highlighter, pen and pencil, and make *this* TCC your own!

- To Peace, Life and Love for Humankind, Antonio Polanco @cinemanyc

American Beauty* **[3]**

✓Toy Story 2*   **Saw it**

A Map of the World

An Ideal Husband

✓Analyze This*@ ← **Watched at the Cinema**

Angela's Ashes

✓Anna and the King ✈
Saw it on a Flight

Anywhere But Here

Being John Malkovich   **Loved it!**

✓Boys Don't Cry

Election   **To Watch Later (Mark in Pencil)**

Girl, Interrupted

Magnolia ★   **Super Favorite!!**

✓Man on the Moon* ◎
Great DVD/Special Features

Music of the Heart

✓Notting Hill* 🧡   **Date Night!**

Sweet and Lowdown

The Cider House Rules*

The End of the Affair

The Green Mile ③   **Saw it 3X**

The Hurricane*

✓The Insider
More Watched @Cinema Suggestions

The Legend of 1900

The Limey %   **Watched some**

The Muse

The Sixth Sense*@^{2} **Saw 2X @Cinema (or 3, 4, more)**

✓The Straight Story
Thought Provoking!

The Talented Mr. Ripley* *MF!*
Mind F#@k

Tumbleweeds

1999 BLOCKBUSTERS

Star Wars: Episode I
The Phantom Menace in *3D!*

A Civil Action 🕐 • • • ➤
Sign ideas to Watch Later

American Pie *Seen it*

Austin Powers: *Loved it!*
The Spy Who Shagged Me

Big Daddy 📺 *Saw it on TV*

Blue Streak

Bowfinger 😆 *Funny!*

Deuce Bigalow: Male Gigolo

Double Jeopardy *Did NOT like it*
☹️ 👎

Entrapment

Forces of Nature

Inspector Gadget 💡 *That gives me*
an Idea!

Life ☐ *To fill in later (free use)*
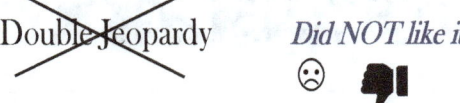
ie. ☒ ☑ ■ ● ◿ Ⓡ ▣

Never Been Kissed ♡ *Lee*
Date Night (w/X)

Payback

Runaway Bride XO *Love Story*

She's All That

South Park: Bigger, Longer & Uncut

Stepmom 🌧️ *Rainy day movie*

The Bone Collector 💀 *Scary!*

The General's Daughter

The Matrix IMAX *or* 4DX

The Mummy *Special screening!*

The Thomas Crown Affair

The World Is Not Enough *007*

Three Kings

Varsity Blues

WAYS TO USE THE CINEPHILE CATALOGUE!

- ✅ Check off every movie you've seen!
- ✅ Highlight your favorite films
- ✅ Add ratings & personal notes
- ✅ Discover new cinema
- ✅ Mark films to watch later
- ✅ Relive magic movie memories
- ✅ Express your inner critic
- ✅ Share it with friends & family
- ✅ Digital edition available

LEGEND REFRESHER

Academy Awards Winners	Golden Globe Winners	Winner of the Palme D'Or	Winner of the BAFTA awards

Highest Grossing Worldwide $$$	Highest Grossing Domestic $	* Box Office Hits	** Blockbuster/ Award Films	*Criterion Collection*

WHAT YOU'LL NEED

- o Pen, Pencil & (*my personal favorite*) Highlighter
  - ▪ If you're sharing with others, I'd recommend each person using a different color highlighter
- o Your beautifully unique movie history!
- o Anything else you might need or use for a journal

FILM FIRSTS

Passage de Venus (1874)	First film footage
Roundhay Garden Scene (1888)	First film, produced by French artist and inventor Louis Le Prince
Monkeyshines (1889-90)	Believed to be the first film shot in America, in the original cylinder kinetograph format
Pope Leo XIII (1890s)	First Pope captured on film
Dickson Greeting aka Monkeyshines 2 (1891)	First public demonstration of motion pictures in the US
Un Bon Bock (1892)	First animated film
Dickson Experimental Sound Film (1894-95)	First sound film
Dorlita in the Passion Dance (1894)	First film banned in the US
The Boxing Cats (1894)	First LOL cat film
Incident at Clovelly Cottage (1895)	First film made in the UK
Leaving the Factory (1895)	*First film shown to an audience *First film made in France

The Arrest of a Pickpocket (1895)	First crime film
The Execution of Mary, Queen of Scots (1895)	First use of camera tricks
The Cabbage Fairy (1896)	*First film directed by a woman, Alice Guy-Blaché who went on to direct 464 short and full length movies *Introduced the use of screenplays
The Coronation of Tsar Nicholas II (1896)	One of the first significant news events caught on film
The House of the Devil (1896)	First horror film
The Kiss (1896)	*First kiss on film *First movie for demanded censorship
After the Ball, the Bath (1897)	First nudity illusion on film
Santa Claus (1898)	First Christmas film
King John (1899)	*First Shakespearean adaptation *First adaptation
The Humpty Dumpty Circus (1899)	First use of object manipulation and stop-motion animation in film

Sherlock Holmes Baffled (1900)	*First mystery film *First Sherlock Holmes film
Scrooge or Marley's Ghost (1901)	First use of intertitles in film
Burnley v Manchester United (1902)	First film with sports
The Great Train Robbery (1903)	*First legitimate box-office hit *First use of multiple camera positions and acceleration editing for a dramatic story
Dream of a Rarebit Fiend (1906)	First spit take in a movie
The Black Hand (1906)	First gangster movie
The Story of the Kelly Gang (1906)	First feature-length film
An Exciting Honeymoon and The Life of a Cowboy (1907)	First film reviews (published by Variety)
A Visit to the Seaside (1908)	First film to use Kinemascope; first film ever made in color
The Assassination of the Duke of Guise (1908)	First film to have a music score written explicitly for it

The Yiddisher Boy (1909)	First flashback in a movie
Dante's Inferno (1911)	First film shown in its entirety in the US
In Old California (1912)	First movie made in Hollywood, CA
Cabiria (1914)	First epic motion picture
The Merchant of Venice (1914)	First feature-length film directed by an American woman, Lois Weber
The Squaw Man (1914)	First western film
Tillie's Punctured Romance (1914)	First feature-length American comedy
Hypocrites (1915)	First film to show full frontal nudity
The Birth of a Nation (1915)	First major controversial motion picture
Fall of a Nation (1916)	First sequel (to *Birth of A Nation*)
Vice Versa (1916)	First body swap film

The Gulf Between (1917)	First Technicolor film
Men Who Have Made Love to Me (1918)	First film to break the 4th wall
The Squaw Man (1918)	First remake
The Cabinet of Dr. Caligari (1920)	First major horror movie
A Connecticut Yankee in King Arthur's Court (1921)	First movie with time travel
Robin Hood (1922)	First movie to have a Hollywood premiere
The Lost World (1922)	*First feature length sci-fi film *First film shown on an airplane (by Imperial Airways)
The Power of Love (1922)	First 3D film, presented with 3D glasses (the movie was not widely released and is currently lost)
The Toll of the Sea (1922)	First Hollywood film to use two strip Technicolor (film entirely in color without the use of a special projector)
The Adventures of Prince Achmed (1926)	First (surviving) animated movie

Napoleon (1927)	First film to be filmed in the widescreen format
The Jazz Singer (1927)	First "talkie" (use of the sound effect)
Wings (1927)	First motion picture to win Best Picture (Academy Awards)
Lights of New York (1928)	First fully sound movie
Steamboat Willie (1928)	*First animated film with sound *First Mickey Mouse cartoon released
Blackmail (1929)	First British sound film
Glorifying the American Girl (1929)	First use of 'damn' in a movie
On With the Show (1929)	First all-talking, all-color film
The Broadway Melody (1929)	First feature full length musical
All Quiet on the Western Front (1930)	First anti-war film
Elstree Calling (1930)	First film to show a TV set

Hell's Angels (1930)	First use of "son of a bitch" in a movie
The Big Trail (1930)	First known movie to use a swear
Dracula (1931)	First film called a "horror movie" (in critics' reviews)
White Zombie (1932)	First zombie movie
Ecstasy (1933)	*First sex scene in a film *First on-screen female orgasm
The Crooked Circle (1933)	First film shown on TV
It Happened One Night (1934)	First film to win the *Big 5* at The Oscars: Best Picture, Best Director, Best Actress, Best Actor, Best Adapted Screenplay
Becky Sharp (1935)	First feature-length Technicolor film
Snow White and the Seven Dwarfs (1937)	First animated movie
Gone With the Wind (1939)	First official Oscar awarded to an African American artist for Best Supporting Actress: Hattie McDaniel

Mandrake, the Magician (1939)	First superhero movie
Fantasia (1940)	First movie with stereo sound
Stranger on the 3rd Floor (1940)	First film noir
Now, Voyager (1942)	First nerdy girl makeover
The Song of Bernadette (1943)	First Best Picture winner at the Golden Globe Awards
The Best Years of Our Lives (1948)	First Best Film winner at the BAFTAS (British Academy Film Awards)
Rashomon (1950)	First direct shot of the sun
Distant Drums (1951)	First film to use the Wilhelm scream
Bwana Devil (1952)	First 3D movie
House of Wax (1953)	First major studio film shot in 3D
The Robe (1953)	First film released in CinemaScope

The War of the Worlds (1953)	First alien invasion film
Marty (1955)	First film awarded the Palme D'Or at the Cannes Film Festival
The Blackboard Jungle (1955)	First film to use rock in a soundtrack
Island in the Sun (1957)	First interracial kiss
Psycho (1960)	First film to show a flushing toilet
The Apartment (1960)	First film released in Panavision
The Manchurian Candidate (1962)	First karate fight on film
Goldfinger (1964)	First film featuring a GPS device
One Potato, Two Potato (1964)	First film to feature an interracial marriage
In Cold Blood (1967)	First use of the word *Bullshit* in a movie
Oliver! (1969)	First G-rated film to win Best Picture (Academy Awards)

Midnight Cowboy (1970)	First X-rated movie to win Best Picture (Academy Awards)
Carnal Knowledge (1971)	First movie to publicize condom usage
Sunday Bloody Sunday (1971)	First mainstream film to present a same-sex/gay kiss
Sweet Sweetback's Baadasssss Song (1971)	First commercially successful blaxploitation film
The Young Teacher (1972)	First movie released on VHS
Westworld (1973)	First Hollywood film to use '2G' CGI
Barry Lyndon (1975)	First film with scenes shot entirely by natural candlelight
Jaws (1975)	First blockbuster, making over $100M in a single release and later collecting $100M in rentals
Star Wars: Episode IV A New Hope (1977)	*A pioneer for visual effects and sci-fi, thanks to Industrial Light & Magic *Also notable for merchandising aspects such as tie-in products and cross-promotion central to profit-making in the film industry

Watership Down (1978)	First animated film presented in Dolby Stereo
The Blues Brothers (1980)	First film based on an SNL sketch
Looker (1981)	First movie to have a CGI character
Rock & Rule (1983)	First animated film to use computer graphics
Star Wars: Episode VI Return of the Jedi (1983)	First film shown in a THX certified auditorium
Red Dawn (1984)	First PG-13 movie
The Sensorium (1984)	Regarded as the world's first 4D film
Lethal Weapon (1987)	First movie to show a character using a cell phone
Robocop 2 (1990)	First feature-length film to use real-time computer graphics
The Rescuers Down Under (1990)	*First fully digital feature film using Disney's 'CAPS' effects system *First Disney theatrical sequel
Beauty and the Beast (1991)	First animated movie nominated for Best Picture (Academy Awards)

Terminator 2: Judgment Day (1991)	First film with a $100M+ budget
Wax or the Discovery of Television Among the Bees (1991)	First film to be streamed online (in 1994)
Batman Returns (1992)	First movie using Dolby Digital sound
Death Becomes Her (1992)	First human skin CGI software in used in a film
Jurassic Park (1993)	First movie using DTS digital sound
The Flintstones (1994)	First CGI-rendered fur in a film
Casper (1995)	First CGI lead character
Party Girl (1995)	First film to premiere on the internet
Toy Story (1995)	First feature-length animated CGI film
The Cable Guy (1996)	First time an actor (Jim Carrey) is paid a $20M salary for a movie role
Twister (1996)	First movie released on DVD

Titanic (1997)	First film to gross $1 billion dollars
O Brother, Where Art Thou? (2000)	First feature film to be entirely color corrected by digital means
Final Fantasy: The Spirits Within (2001)	First feature film to use motion capture to create characters
Shrek (2001)	First ever winner for Best Animated Feature (Academy Awards)
Spirited Away (2001)	First anime film to win Best Animated Feature (Academy Awards)
Russian Ark (2002)	*First feature film to be shot entirely in uncompressed high-definition video *First feature film to consist of a single unedited take
Star Wars: Episode II Attack of the Clones (2002)	First major movie shot entirely on digital film
The Polar Express (2004)	First CGI movie that used motion capture for all actors
Sky Captain and the World of Tomorrow (2004)	First film shot entirely with a digital background
A History of Violence (2005)	Last movie widely released on VHS

Memoirs Of A Geisha (2005)	First all-Asian Hollywood cast
Sex Drive (2008)	First US film to use on-screen texting
U2 3D (2008)	*First live-action film to be shot, posted and exhibited entirely in 3D *First live-action digital 3D film *First 3D concert film
Avatar (2009)	First 3D film to become the highest grossing film of all time ($2.847B)
Monsters vs. Aliens (2009)	First animated film to be directly produced in the stereoscopic 3D format instead of being converted into 3D after completion
Toy Story 3 (2010)	First animated film to cost at least $20M, and also the first animated film to gross over a $1B
The Hobbit: An Unexpected Journey (2012)	First wide-release film to be shot using a high frame rate (shot at 48 frames per second, twice the usual 24 frames per second)
Frankenweenie (2012)	First black-and-white film and the first stop-motion animated film to be released in IMAX
Skyfall (2013)	First film to gross over £100 million in the United Kingdom

The Wolf of Wall Street (2013)	First major American movie delivered to theaters in digital formats only
Parasite (2019)	First film to win the Oscar for Best Picture and Best Foreign Film
The Lion King (2019)	First fully CGI "live action" movie
Witch Tales (2019)	*First horror anthology feature movie filmed simultaneously in Spanish and English languages *Released respectively as *Witch Tales* and *Cuentos de la Bruja*
Nomadland (2020)	First Oscar Best Picture winning film to be released theatrically, direct-to-streaming and VOD at the same time
The Suicide Squad (2021)	*First non-Marvel Studios film to be shot entirely with IMAX-certified digital cameras *First feature film to use the Red Komodo camera (also shot with the Red Ranger Monstro 8K & Komodo 6K cameras)
The Tomorrow War (2021)	First streaming original film to cost c. $200 million to produce (originally set for a theatrical release by Paramount Pictures)
Oppenheimer (2023)	First film to shoot sections in IMAX black and white analog photography

The Creator (2023)	First large-budget major studio film to be shot on the prosumer Sony FX3 camera, the low cost of which is a rarity for a blockbuster film

TOP LIFETIME GROSSING FILMS (AS OF AUG 2024)

Avatar	$2.92B	Top Gun Maverick	$1.5B
Avengers: Endgame	$2.8B	Frozen II	$1.45B
Avatar: The Way of Water	$2.3B	Barbie	$1.45B
Titanic	$2.26B	Frozen	$1.39B
Star Wars: Episode VII The Force Awakens	$2.07B	The Super Mario Bros. Movie	$1.36B
Avengers: Infinity War	$2.05B	Harry Potter and the Deathly Hallows: Part 2	$1.34B
Spider-Man: No Way Home	$1.9B	Black Panther	$1.35B
Jurassic World	$1.67B	Star Wars: The Last Jedi	$1.3B
The Lion King (2019)	$1.66B	Jurassic World: Fallen Kingdom	$1.3B
Inside Out 2	$1.65B	Beauty and the Beast (2017)	$1.26B
Avengers: Age of Ultron	$1.54B	Incredibles 2	$1.24B
Furious 7	$1.5B	The Fate of the Furious	$1.23B
The Avengers (2012)	$1.52B	Iron Man 3	$1.2B

Deadpool & Wolverine $1.22B

The Lord of the Rings:
The Return of the King $1.18B

Minions $1.16B

Aquaman $1.15B

Captain America: Civil War $1.15B

Skyfall $1.14B

Spider-Man Far From Home $1.13B

Captain Marvel $1.13B

Transformers: Dark of the Moon $1.1B

Jurassic Park $1.1B

The Dark Knight Rises $1.1B

The Lord of the Rings:
The Two Towers $1.1B

Transformers: Age of Extinction $1.1B

Joker $1.08B

Star Wars: The Rise of Skywalker
$1.07B

Toy Story 4 $1.07B

Toy Story 3 $1.06B

Pirates of the Caribbean:
Dead Man's Chest $1.06B

Rogue One: A Star Wars Story $1.06B

Aladdin (2019) $1.05B

Harry Potter and the Sorcerer's Stone
$1.05B

Pirates of the Caribbean:
On Stranger Tides $1.04B

Despicable Me 3 $1.03B

Zootopia $1.03B

The Dark Knight $1.03B

Star Wars: The Phantom Menace
$1.029B

GENRES

AWARD SEASON

BLOCKBUSTERS

CRITICALLY ACCLAIMED

DOCUMENTARIES

ANIMATED SHORT

FOR THE FAMILY & KIDS

FOREIGN FILMS

HONORABLE MENTION

HORROR & CULT

NEW MEDIA/MADE FOR TV

RATED X

THIS MOVIE SUCKS

1989 AWARD SEASON

Born on the Fourth of July*

Dead Poets Society*

Driving Miss Daisy*   [2]

A Dry White Season

Crimes and Misdemeanors

Do the Right Thing*

Drugstore Cowboy

Field of Dreams*

Glory*

Henry V

Jacknife

Last Exit to Brooklyn

Music Box

My Left Foot

Mystery Train

Sea of Love*

Sex Lies and Videotape

Shirley Valentine

The Fabulous Baker Boys

The Unbelievable Truth

The War of the Roses*

True Love

When Harry Met Sally…*

BLOCKBUSTERS

Batman

Indiana Jones
and the Last Crusade

Always

Back to the Future Part II

Bill & Ted's Excellent Adventure

Black Rain

Fletch Lives

Ghostbusters II

Harlem Nights

K-9

Lethal Weapon 2

License to Kill

Look Who's Talking

Major League

Road House

Say Anything...

Star Trek V: The Final Frontier

Steel Magnolias

Tango & Cash

The Abyss

The Bear

The Karate Kid Part III

Three Fugitives

Turner & Hooch

Uncle Buck

Weekend at Bernie's

CRITICALLY ACCLAIMED

Casualties of War

Parenthood

Dad

Roe V. Wade

How to Get Ahead in Advertising

She-Devil

In Country

Tap

Lady in the Corner

The Mighty Quinn

Lean on Me

UHF

National Lampoon's
Christmas Vacation

DOCUMENTARIES

Common Threads:
Stories from The Quilt

Lost Children of the Empire

Roger & Me

Adam Clayton Powell

Crack USA: Country Under Siege

Super Chief:
The Life and Legacy of Earl Warren

Depeche Mode 101

Viewpoint 89: Cambodia Year 10

For All Mankind

FOR THE FAMILY & KIDS

All Dogs Go to Heaven*

Asterix and the Big Fight

Babar: The Movie

Cheetah

Granpa

Honey, I Shrunk the Kids*

Kiki's Delivery Service

Little Monsters

Little Nemo:
Adventures in Slumberland

Looking for Miracles

Prancer*

The Adventures of Chatran

The BFG

The Little Mermaid*

The Wizard*

FOREIGN FILMS

A City of Sadness   TAI

Black Rain   JPN

Interrogation   POL

Jesus of Montreal   CAN

Life and Nothing But   FR

Mama, There's a Man
in Your Bed   FR

My Heart is That Eternal Rose   HK

Revenge   USSR

Sweetie   AUT

The Aesthetic Syndrome   USSR

The Cook, The Thief, His Wife
& Her Lover   NLD/UK/FR

The Killer   HK

The Power of
Kangwon Province   KOR

The Seventh Continent   AUS

The Winter War   FIN

Tie Me Up! Tie Me Down! SPA

Traffik   UK

Violent Cop   JPN

Waltzing Regitze   DNK

What Happened to Santiago PR

Zatoichi: Darkness is His Ally   JPN

HONORABLE MENTION

84C MoPic

In the Aftermath

Bert Rigby, You're a Fool

Johnny Handsome

Blind Fury

Resurrected

Bloodhounds of Broadway

See No Evil, Hear No Evil

Chattahoochee

Signs of Life

Cousins

Spirits of the Air,
Gremlins of the Clouds

Double Your Pleasure

The Dream Team

Earth Girls Are Easy

The Penthouse

Fat Man & Little Boy

Under the Boardwalk

Gross Anatomy

High Stakes

HORROR & CULT

A Nightmare on Elm Street
Part 5: The Dream Child*

Blood Red

Bride of Re-Animator

Dead Calm

Dr. Calipari

Godzilla v. Biollante

Friday the 13th Part VIII:
Jason Takes Manhattan*

Halloween 5:
The Revenge of Michael Myers*

Leviathan

Life is Cheap…
But Toilet Paper is Expensive

Marquis

Meet the Feebles

Midnight

Parents

Pet Sematary*

Phantom of the Mall:
Eric's Revenge

Puppet Master

Santa Sangre

Society

Sundown: The Vampire in Retreat

Tetsuo: The Iron Man

The 'Burbs*

The Fly II*

MADE FOR TV

War and Remembrance   UK

Out on the Edge

Lonesome Dove

The Women of Brewster Place

My Name is Bill W.

THIS MOVIE SUCKS

Bye Bye Baby

Old Gringo

Ghosts Can't Do It

Speed Zone!

Heart of Dixie

The Return of Swamp Thing

Her Alibi

Things

Listen to Me

Wild Orchid

Lock Up

Wired

<u>NOTES</u>

Your All Time Favorite Film?

1988 AWARD SEASON

Rain Man* [2]

Working Girl*

A Fish Called Wanda*

Beaches

Big*

Biloxi Blues*

Bull Durham

Dangerous Liaisons*

Distant Voice, Still Lives

Evil Angels
A Cry in the Dark

Gorillas in the Mist*

Madame Sousatzka

Married to the Mob

Midnight Run*

Mississippi Burning*

Mystic Pizza

Running on Empty

Stand and Deliver

Stormy Monday

The Accidental Tourist*

The Accused*

The Last Temptation of Christ

The Unbearable Lightness of Being

1988

BLOCKBUSTERS

Who Framed Roger Rabbit **

Above the Law

Alien Nation

Beetlejuice

Betrayed

Big Business

Caddyshack II

Cocktail

Colors

Coming to America

Crocodile Dundee II

Die Hard

Dirty Rotten Scoundrels

Funny Farm

Rambo III

Red Heat

Scrooged

Short Circuit 2

Shoot to Kill

Tequila Sunrise

The Dead Pool

The Great Outdoors

The Naked Gun:
From the Files of Police Squad!

Tucker: The Man and His Dream

Twins

Willow

Young Guns

CRITICALLY ACCLAIMED

Bird

Buster

Crossing Delancey

Dominick & Eugene

Grave of the Fireflies

I'm Gonna Git You Sucka!

Moon Over Parador

My Neighbor Totoro

School Daze

Tanner '88

The Adventures of Baron Munchausen

*The Qatsi Trilogy 2: Powaqqatsi:
Life in Transformation*

DOCUMENTARIES

Hotel Terminus: The Life
and Times of Klaus Barbie

In from the Cold:
A Portrait of Richard Burton

Let's Get Lost

Promises to Keep

Radio Bikini

The Cry of Reason – Beyers Naude:
An Afrikaner Speaks Out

The Duty Men: East Enders

The Thin Blue Line

This Week: Death on the Rock

Viewpoint Special:
The Man Who Killed Kennedy

FOR THE FAMILY & KIDS

BraveStarr: The Movie

Care Bears Nutcracker Suite

Daffy Duck's Quackbusters

David and the Magic Pearl

Ernest Saves Christmas*

Felix the Cat: The Movie

Just Ask for Diamond

Oliver & Company

Purple People Eater

Rockin' with Judy Jetson

Scooby-Doo and the Ghoul School

The Good, the Bad, and Huckleberry Hound

The Land Before Time*

The New Adventures of Pippi Longstocking

Willy the Sparrow

Yogi and the Invasion of the Space Bears

FOREIGN FILMS

Cinema Paradiso   IT   **[2]**

A Tale of the Wind   FR

Apartment Zero   UK

Ariel   FIN

Camille Claudel   FR

Drowning by Numbers   UK/NTL

Ghosts… of the Civil Dead   AUS

Hanussen   HUN

Landscape in the Mist   GRC

My Uncle's Legacy   YUG

Police Story 2   HK

Salaam Bombay!   IND

Story of Women   FR

The Decalogue   POL

The Music Teacher   BEL

The Navigator:
A Medieval Odyssey   AUS/NZL

Time of Violence   BUL

Women on the Verge of a
Nervous Breakdown   SPA

HONORABLE MENTION

A Handful of Dust

Action Jackson

Big Top Pee-Wee

Bloodsport

Cocoon: The Return

License to Drive

Punchline

The Milagro Beanfield War

The Presidio

HORROR & CULT

976-EVIL

A Nightmare on Elm Street
Part 4: The Dream Master*

Akira

Cane Toads: An Unnatural
History on the Silver Globe

Child's Play*

Dead Ringers

Dream Demon

Elvira, Mistress of The Dark

Friday the 13th Part VII:
The New Blood*

Halloween 4:
The Return of Michael Myers*

Heathers*

Hellbound: Hellraiser II

High Spirits

Killer Klowns From Outer Space

Maniac Cop

Night of the Demons

Poltergeist III*

Return of the Living Dead 2

Tales from the Gimli Hospital

Tape Heads

The Blob

The Lair of the White Worm

The Serpent and the Rainbow

The Seventh Sign*

The Vanishing

They Live

Two Moon Junction

Vampire's Kiss

Waxwork

MADE FOR TV

Baby M	The Ann Jillian Story
Baja Oklahoma	The Bourne Identity
Hemingway	The Murder of Mary Phagan
Jack the Ripper	The Tenth Man
Lincoln	The Woman He Loved

THIS MOVIE SUCKS

And God Created Woman	Mortuary Academy
Arthur 2: On the Rocks	Police Academy 5: Assignment Miami Beach
Hobgoblins	
	Sleepaway Camp 2: Unhappy Campers
Hot to Trot	
	Sunset
Johnny Be Good	
	Switching Channels
Mac and Me	
	The Telephone

<u>NOTES</u>

Best guess, how many movies have you watched in your Life?

1987 AWARD SEASON

Hope and Glory

*The Last Emperor** **[3]**

Anna

Baby Boom

*Broadcast News**

Cry Freedom

Dirty Dancing*

Empire of the Sun

Full Metal Jacket*

Gaby: A True Story

Good Morning, Vietnam

Ironwood

*La Bamba**

Mannequin

Matewan

Moonstruck*

Nuts

Outrageous Fortune

Radio Days

Street Smart

The Dead

*The Princess Bride**

The Untouchables*

The Whales of August

The Witches of Eastwick*

Throw Momma from the Train*

Wall Street*

BLOCKBUSTERS

Fatal Attraction **

Three Men and a Baby

Adventures in Babysitting

*Batteries Not Included

Benjy the Hunted

Beverly Hills Cop II

Black Widow

Blind Date

Can't Buy Me Love

Dragnet

Harry and the Hendersons

Lethal Weapon

Overboard

Planes, Trains and Automobiles

Predator

Raising Arizona

Revenge of the Nerds II:
Nerds in Paradise

Robocop

Roxanne

Spaceballs

Stakeout

Summer School

The Living Daylights

The Running Man

The Secret of My Success

Tin Men

Who's That Girl

CRITICALLY ACCLAIMED

Bagdad Café

Made in Heaven

Barfly

Neo-Tokyo

Border Radio

Penitentiary III

Bulletproof

The Glass Menagerie

Hollywood Shuffle

Walker

House of Games

Withnail & I

Innerspace

DOCUMENTARIES

The Ten-Year Lunch:
The Wit and Legend of
the Algonquin Round Table

Forty Minutes: Home from the Hill

Fourteen Days in May

A Stitch for Time

Man-Eating Tigers/Saving the Tiger

Baka People of the People

Who Killed Vincent Chin?

Eyes on the Prize: America's Civil
Rights Years/Bridge to Freedom
1965

FOR THE FAMILY & KIDS

Ernest Goes to Camp*

G.I. Joe: The Movie*

Mio in the Land of Faraway

The Brave Little Toaster

The Chipmunk Adventure

The Great Land of Small

The Jetsons Meet the Flintstones

The Puppetoon Movie

The Secret Garden

Top Cat and the Beverly Hills Cats

Where is the Friend's House?

Yogi's Great Escape

FOREIGN FILMS

Babette's Feast   DNK

Pelle the Conqueror DNK **[3]**

Under the Sun of Satan   FR

38 Vienna Before the Fall   GER

84 Charing Cross Road   UK

A Chinese Ghost Story   HK

A Taxing Woman   JPN

Course Completed   SPA

Dark Eyes   IT

Europa 2: Epidemic   DAN

Goodbye, Children   FR

Little Dorrit   UK

Maurice   UK

Pathfinder   NOR

Prick Up Your Ears   UK

Project A Part II   HK

Red Sorghum   CH

Repentance   USSR

The Emperor's Naked Army
Marches On   JPN

The Family   IT

Wings of Desire   GER

HORROR & CULT

A Nightmare on Elm Street
Part 3: Dream Warriors*

Angel Heart

Blood Diner

Creepshow 2*

Death Line

Dolls

Evil Dead 2: Dead by Dawn

Gandahar

House 2: The Second Story

Housekeeping

Lady in White

Near Dark

Nekromantik

Prince of Darkness

Prison	The Cure for Insomnia
Stagefright	The Gate
Street Trash	The Kindred
Tales From the Quadead Zone	The Lost Boys*
The Believers	The Outing

MADE FOR TV

Escape From Sobibor	In Love and War
Poor Little Rich Girl: The Barbara Hutton Story	LBJ: The Early Years
After The Promise	Long Day's Journey into Night
Amerika	Right to Die
Billionaire Boys Club	Sworn to Silence
Echoes in the Darkness	The Betty Ford Story
	The Two Mrs. Grenvilles
Foxfire	

THIS MOVIE SUCKS

Aenigma

Disorderlies

From the Hip

Ishtar

Jaws: The Revenge*

Leonard Part 6

Masters of the Universe*

Million Dollar Mystery

Nukie

Over the Top

Police Academy 4:
Citizens on Patrol*

Rent-a-Cop

Siesta

Silent Night, Deadly Night Part 2

Superman IV:
The Quest for Peace*

Surf Nazis Must Die

The Barbarians

The Garbage Pail Kids Movie*

Three Bewildered People
in the Night

Tough Guys Don't Dance

<u>NOTES</u>

If your Life was a major motion picture, what would it be called?

1986 AWARD SEASON

Hannah and Her Sisters

Platoon*   [2]

The Mission

At Close Range

Blue Velvet

Children of a Lesser God

Crimes of the Heart

Crocodile Dundee*

Defense of the Real

Down and Out in Beverly Hills*

Down by Law

Duet for One

Extremities

Little Shop of Horrors*

Mona Lisa

Night Mother

Peggy Sue Got Married*

'Round Midnight

Sid and Nancy

Something Wild

Stand by Me*

The Color of Money*

The Mosquito Coast

True Stories

BLOCKBUSTERS

Top Gun **

An American Tail

Back to School

Big Trouble in Little China

Cobra

F/X

Ferris Bueller's Day Off

Heartbreak Ridge

Jo Jo Dancer, Your Life Is Calling

Labyrinth

Legal Eagles

Police Academy 3: Back in Training

Pretty in Pink

Ruthless People

Short Circuit

Star Trek IV: The Voyage Home

The Fly

The Golden Child

The Karate Kid Part II

The Money Pit

Three Amigos!

Tough Guys

CRITICALLY ACCLAIMED

9 1/2 Weeks

Salvador

Highlander

She's Gotta Have It

Hoosiers

Wildcats

Jumpin' Jack Flash

Working Girls

DOCUMENTARIES

Down and Out in America

Isaac in America

Chile: Hasta Cuando?

Witness to Apartheid

Hellfire: A Journey from Hiroshima

FOR THE FAMILY & KIDS

Babes in Toyland

Care Bears Movie II:
A New Generation

Castle in the Sky

Flight of the Navigator

GoBots: Battle of the Rock Lords

Heathcliff: The Movie

Laputa

Momo

My Little Pony: The Movie

SpaceCamp

Super Mario Bros: The Movie

The Adventures of Milo and Otis

The Great Mouse Detective*

Transformers: The Movie*

FOREIGN FILMS

Jean de Florette   FR/SWZ/IT

The Assault   NLD   [2]

The Sacrifice   SWE/UK/FR

Avanti Popolo   ISR

Bashu, the Little Stranger   IRN

Betty Blue   FR

Ginger and Fred   IT

In a Glass Cage   SPA

Kin-Dza-Dza! USSR

Manon des Sources   FR

Matador   SPA

Millionaire Express   CH

Otello   IT

Peking Opera Blues   HK

The Decline of the American Empire CAN

The Horse Thief   CH

The Legend of Suram Fortress   SOV

The Name of the Rose IT/GER/FR

To Sleep So as To Dream   JPN

HONORABLE MENTION

Allan Quatermain
and the Lost City of Gold

Gung Ho

Heartburn

Howard the Duck

Iron Eagle

Nothing in Common

Running Scared

The Morning After

Youngblood

HORROR & CULT

Aliens*

Class of Nuke 'Em High

Demons 2

Devil in the Flesh

Friday the 13th Part VI:
Jason Lives*

From Beyond

Gothic

Henry: Portrait of a Serial Killer

House

Mindhunter

Neon Maniacs

Poltergeist II: The Other Side*

Psycho III*

The Texas Chainsaw Massacre 2

Vamp

MADE FOR TV

Promise

Nobody's Child

Anastasia: The Mystery of Anna

Peter the Great

Christmas Eve

The Deliberate Stranger

Nazi Hunter:
The Beate Klarsfeld Story

Unnatural Causes

THIS MOVIE SUCKS

American Anthem

Maximum Overdrive

Blue City

Power

Chopping Mall

Ratboy

Club Paradise

Shanghai Surprise

Haunted Honeymoon

Soul Man

Invaders from Mars

That's Life

King Kong Lives

Under the Cherry Moon

<u>NOTES</u>

What's your favorite movie series? Favorite film franchise?

A Room with a View

Out of Africa*   [2]

Prizzi's Honor*

The Purple Rose of Cairo

A Chorus Line

Agnes of God

Brazil

Cocoon*

Desperately Seeking Susan*

Jagged Edge*

Kiss of the Spider Woman*

Ladyhawke*

Lost in America

Louie Blue

Murphy's Romance*

Pale Ride

Runaway Train

The Color Purple*

The Emerald Forest*

The Trip to Bountiful

Twice in a Lifetime

White Nights*

Witness*

BLOCKBUSTERS

Back to the Future **

Pee-Wee's Big Adventure

A View to a Kill

Police Academy 2:
Their First Assignment

Better Off Dead

Porky's Revenge

Brewster's Millions

Rambo: First Blood Part II

Commando

Real Genius

Death Wish 3

Rocky IV

Fletch

Silverado

Legend

Spies Like Us

Mad Max Beyond Thunderdome

St. Elmo's Fire

Mask

Summer Rental

National Lampoon's
European Vacation

Teen Wolf

Pale Rider

The Breakfast Club

The Goonies

The Jewel of the Nile

The Last Dragon

Weird Science

Young Sherlock Holmes

CRITICALLY ACCLAIMED

After Hours

Dim Sum: A Little Bit of Heart

Flesh and Blood

Girls Just Want to Have Fun

King Solomon's Mines

Krush Groove

Mala Noche

Red Sonja

To Live and Die in L.A.

Turk 182

Year of the Dragon

DOCUMENTARIES

28 Up

Shoah

Artie Shaw: Time is All You've Got

Soldiers in Hiding

Broken Rainbow

Stripper

In the Name of the People

The Statue of Liberty

FOR THE FAMILY & KIDS

Asterix Versus Caesar

Sesame Street Presents
Follow That Bird

D.A.R.Y.L.

The Adventures of Mark Twain

He-Man and She-Ra:
The Secret of the Sword

The Black Cauldron

Here Come the Littles

The Care Bears Movie

Rainbow Brite and the Star Stealer

The Dirt Bike Kid

Return to Oz

The Peanut Butter Solution

Santa Claus: The Movie*

The Pickwick Papers

FOREIGN FILMS

My Life as a Dog   SWE

Ran   JPN

The Killing Fields   UK

The Official Story   ARG   **[2]**

When Father Was Away on
Business   YUG

A Time to Live
and a Time to Die   TAI

Angry Harvest   GER

Colonel Redl   HUN

Fire Festival   JPN

Insignificance   UK

Mishima:
A Life in Four Chapters US/JPN

My Beautiful Launderette   UK

My Friend Ivan Lapshin   USSR

My Lucky Stars   HK

My Sweet Little Village   CZE

Police Story   HK

Subway   FR

Taipei Story   TAI

Tampopo   JPN

The Quiet Earth   NZL

The Woman and the Stranger   GER

Three Men and a Cradle   FR

Vagabond   FR/UK

Wetherby   UK

HONORABLE MENTION

Code of Silence

The Falcon and the Snowman

Invasion U.S.A.

The Sure Thing

Remo Williams:
The Adventure Begins

Volunteers

Walking the Edge

Revolution

HORROR & CULT

A Nightmare on Elm Street
Part 2: Freddy's Revenge*

Fright Night*

Godzilla 1985: The Legend is Reborn

A Zed & Two Naughts

Night on the Galactic Express

Angel's Egg

Night Train to Terror

Come and See

Ninja Champion

Crime Wave

Phenomena

Day of the Dead

Re-Animator

Friday the 13th Part V:
A New Beginning*

Screamplay

The Bride

The Return of the Living Dead

The Stuff

Vampire Hunter D

MADE FOR TV

The Jewel in the Crown

A Time to Live

Amos

An Early Frost

Consenting Adults

Death of a Salesman

Do You Remember Love?

Kane & Abel

The Rape of Richard Beck

Wallenberg: A Hero's Story

NOTES

What film have you rewatched the most? How many times?

1984 AWARD SEASON

Amadeus   [2]

Romancing the Stone*

2010: The Year We Make Contact*

A Soldier's Story

Beverly Hills Cop*

Blood Simple

Broadway Danny Rose

Choose Me

Country

Micki + Maude*

Moscow on the Hudson*

Mrs. Soffel

Once Upon a Time in America

Places in the Heart

Splash*

Starman

The Bounty

The Cotton Club

The Natural

The Neverending Story

The River

The Woman in Red

BLOCKBUSTERS

Ghostbusters **

Indiana Jones and the
Temple of Doom

Bachelor Party

Breakin'

Breakin' 2: Electric Boogaloo

Cannonball Run II

City Heat

Footloose

Gremlins

Greystoke

Police Academy

Protocol

Red Dawn

Revenge of the Nerds

Sixteen Candles

Star Trek III: The Search for Spock

Supergirl

Teachers

The Adventures of Buckaroo
Bonzai in the 8th Dimension

The Gods Must Be Crazy

The Karate Kid

The Last Starfighter

The Terminator

Tightrope

CRITICALLY ACCLAIMED

1984	*Secret Honor*
All of Me	Songwriter
Blame It on Rio	Swing Shift
Conan The Destroyer	The Bostonians
Garbo Talks	*The Runner*
Love Streams	*This is Spinal Tap*
Purple Rain*	*Under the Volcano*
Repo Man	

DOCUMENTARIES

The Times of Harvey Milk	Marlene
Antonio Gaudi	Stop Making Sense
High Schools	*Streetwise*

FOR THE FAMILY & KIDS

Caravan of Courage:
An Ewok Adventure

The Dog Who Stopped the War

The Muppets Take Manhattan*

Gallavants

The Old Curiosity Shop

Nausicaä of the Valley of the Wind

The Tale of Tsar Saltan

Ronia, the Robber's Daughter

Where the Toys Come From

Super Dimension Fortress Macross:
Do You Remember Love?

FOREIGN FILMS

A Passage to India   UK

Aces Go Places 3   HK

Dangerous Moves   SWZ

Annie's Coming Out   AUS

Beyond the Walls   ISR

Paris, Texas   FR/GER/US

Camilia   ARG

A Private Function   UK

Carmen   FR

A Sunday in the Country   FR

Double Feature   SPA

A Year of the Quiet Sun   POL

Marche a L'ombre   FR

Sexmission   POL

Swann in Love   FR/GER

The Element of Crime/Europa 1
DNK

The Funeral   JPN

The Hit   UK

The Home and The World   IND

Tohfa   IND

HORROR & CULT

A Nightmare on Elm Street*

Delta Space Mission

Dreamscape

Dune

Friday the 13th Part IV:
The Final Chapter*

Give My Regards to Broad St.

Heavenly Bodies

Irreconcilable Differences

Night of the Comet

Ninja III: The Domination

Nothing Lasts Forever

Razorback

Stranger Than Paradise

The Brother from Another Planet

The Toxic Avenger

Voyage of the Rock Aliens

MADE FOR TV

Something About Amelia

Nancy Astor

A Christmas Carol

Sakharov

A Streetcar Named Desire

The Burning Bed

Ellis Island

The Dollmaker

Fatal Vision

THIS MOVIE SUCKS

Body Rock

Savage Streets

Bolero

Sheena

Harry & Son

Slapstick of Another Kind

Night Patrol

Streets of Fire

Rhinestone

Thief of Hearts

Sahara

Where the Boys Are '84

Savage Island

White Fire

NOTES

Do you prefer going to the movies or watching them at home?

1983 AWARD SEASON

Terms of Endearment* [2]

Star 80

Yentl

Tender Mercies

Flashdance*

Testament

Gorky Park

The Big Chill

Heart Like a Wheel

The Dresser

Meantime

The Outsiders

Never Say Never Again

The Pirates of Penzance

Reuben, Reuben

The Right Stuff*

Risky Business

The Star Chamber

Rumble Fish

To Be or Not to Be

Scarface

Trading Places*

Silkwood

Zelig

BLOCKBUSTERS

Star Wars: Episode VI
Return of the Jedi **

A Christmas Story

Breathless

Class

Easy Money

High Road to China

Lone Wolf McQuade

Max Dugan Returns

Mr. Mom

Monty Python's The Meaning of Life

My Tutor

National Lampoon's Vacation

Never Cry Wolf

Octopussy

Porky's II: The Next Day

Revenge of the Ninja

Spacehunter:
Adventures in the Forbidden Zone

Spring Break

Staying Alive

Still Smokin'

Sudden Impact

The Survivors

Twilight Zone: The Movie

Uncommon Valor

Valley Girl

WarGames

CRITICALLY ACCLAIMED

All the Right Moves	Get Crazy
Blue Thunder	Krull
Cross Creek	Under Fire
D.C. Cab	

DOCUMENTARIES

He Makes Me Feel Like Dancin'	Seeing Red
Burroughs: The Movie	Sunless
Children of Darkness	The Profession of Arms
First Contact	The Visit Part III: The Boy David
Forty Minutes: Female Circumcision	*Up*
Schindler	Wildlife on One: Night Life

FOR THE FAMILY & KIDS

Coolie

Phar Lap

Daffy Duck's Fantastic Island

The Black Stallion Returns

Dot and the Bunny

The Wind in the Willows

Mickey's Christmas Carol

Twice Upon a Time

FOREIGN FILMS

Educating Rita   UK

El Norte   US/UK

The Ballad of Narayama   JPN

Entre Nous   FR

Aces Go Places 2   HK

Fearless Hyena II   HK

And The Ship Sales On   IT

Heat and Dust   UK

Barefoot Gem   JPN

Holy Flame of the
Martial World   HK

Carmen   SPA

Le Bal   ALG

Confidentially Yours   FR

Le Derier Combat   FR

Danton   FR

Local Hero   UK

Merry Christmas, Mr. Lawrence
UK/JPN

Money   FR

Prenom Carmen   FR

Project A   HK

The Family Game   JPN

The Fourth Man   NTL

The Makioka Sisters   JPN

The Revolt of Job   HUN

To Our Loves   FR

Urusei Yatsura: Only You   JPN

Wartime Romance   USSR

Zu: Warriors from
the Magic Mountain   NZL

HORROR & CULT

Angst

Brainstorm

Christine*

Cujo*

Curtains

Dimensions of Dialogue

Fear

Golgo 13: The Professional

Nostalgia

Psycho II*

Red Spell Spells Red

Seeding of a Ghost

1983

The Boxer's Omen

The Dead Zone*

The Deadly Spawn

The Hunger

The Keep

Videodrome

MADE FOR TV

The Thorn Birds

Blood Feud

Heart of Steel

Kennedy

Sadat

Special Bulletin

The Day After

The Gift of Love:
A Christmas Story

The Hasty Heart

The Winds of War

Thursday's Child

Who Will Love My Children?

Will There Really Be a Morning?

<u>THIS MOVIE SUCKS</u>

A Night in Heaven

Chained Heat

Fantasy Mission Force

Hercules

Jaws 3D*

Private School… for Girls

Sleepaway Camp

Stranger Invaders

Stroker Ace*

Superman III*

The Lonely Lady

Two of a Kind*

Yor, the Hunter from the Future

<u>NOTES</u>

Do you have a favorite movie house?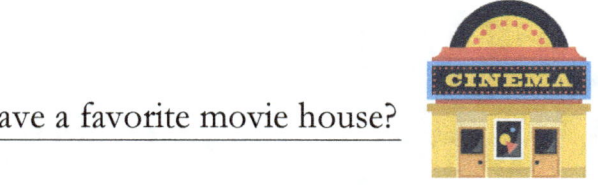

1982 AWARD SEASON

Gandhi*   [3]

Tootsie*

48 Hours*

An Officer and a Gentleman*

Annie*

Author! Author!

Best Friends

Blade Runner*

Cat People

Come Back to the Five and Dime, Jimmy Dean, Jimmy Dean

Diner

Fast Times at Ridgemont High

Frances

Kiss Me Goodbye

Love Child

Missing

My Favorite Year

Night Shift

Shoot the Moon

Sophie's Choice*

Tempest

Tex

The Best Little Whorehouse in Texas*

The Verdict*

The World According to Garp

The Year of Living Dangerously

Victor/Victoria*

BLOCKBUSTERS

E.T. the Extra-Terrestrial

Airplane II: The Sequel

Conan the Barbarian

Creepshow

Dead Men Don't Wear Plaid

Death Wish II

Firefox

First Blood

Grease 2

Poltergeist

Quest for Fire

Richard Pryor:
Life on the Sunset Strip

Rocky III

Six Pack

Some Kind of Hero

Star Trek II:
The Wrath of Khan

The Dark Crystal

The Man from Snowy River

The Road Warrior

The Sword and the Sorcerer

The Toy

They Call Me Bruce

Things Are Tough All Over

TRON

Young Doctors in Love

CRITICALLY ACCLAIMED

Eating Raoul

Koyaanishqatsi: Life Out of Balance

Losing Ground

One From the Heart

Pink Floyd: The Wall

Smithereens

The Ballad of Gregorio Cortez

The King of Comedy

White Dog

DOCUMENTARIES

Beastie Boys:
Video Anthology 1982-2000

Burden of Dreams

Not a Love Story:
A Film About Pornography

The Atomic Café

The Weavers: Wasn't That a Time!

FOR THE FAMILY & KIDS

Aladdin and the Magic Lamp

Bugs Bunny's 3rd Movie:
1001 Rabbit Tales

Friend or Foe

Heidi's Song

Mighty Mouse
in the Great Space Chase

Oliver Twist

The Flight of Dragons

The Last Unicorn

The Secret of NIMH*

FOREIGN FILMS

Fanny and Alexander   SWE   **[2]**

To Begin Again   SPA

Yol / The Way   TUR

A Room in Town   FR

Alsino and the Condor   NIC

Ascendancy   UK

Begin in the Beguine   SPA

Boat People   HK

BRD Trilogy II:
Veronika Voss   GER

Disco Dancer   IND

Dragon Lord   HK

Fitzcarraldo   GER

1982

Flight of the Eagle   SWE

I Are You, You Am Me   JPN

Identification of a Woman   IT

La Traviata   IT

Moonlighting   UK

Private Life   USSR

Querelle   FR/GER

The Beehive   SPA

The Grey Fox   CAN

The Night of the Shooting Stars   IT

The Return of Martin Guerre   FR

The Shaolin Temple   CH/HK

The State of Things   GER

Vidhaata   IND

HONORABLE MENTION

A Question of Silence

Chan is Missing

Hey Good Lookin'

Penitentiary II

The Draughtman's Contract

HORROR & CULT

Alone in the Dark

Q: The Winged Serpent

Amityville II: The Possession

Swamp Thing

Basket Case

Tenebrae

Friday the 13th Part III*

The Entity

Halloween 3: Season of the Witch

The New York Ripper

Himala

The Plague Dogs

Liquid Sky

The Slumber Party Massacre

Manhattan Baby

The Thing

MADE FOR TV

A Woman Called Golda

Made in Britain

Eleanor, First Lady of the World

Mae West

In the Custody of Strangers

The Elephant Man

Life of the Party

The Executioner's Song

1982

The Letter

Too Early/Too Late

The Story of Beatrice

Two of a Kind

THIS MOVIE SUCKS

A Midsummer Night's Sex Comedy

Six Weeks

Angie

The Man Who Saved the World

Butterfly

The Pirate Movie

Deathtrap

The Seduction

Honkytonk Man

Yes, Giorgio

Megaforce

Zapped!

Paradise

<u>NOTES</u>

What's your most memorable movie theater experience?

1981 AWARD SEASON

Arthur*

Chariots of Fire*   [2]

On Golden Pond*

Absence of Malice*

An American Werewolf in London*

Atlantic City

Blow Out

Body Heat

Endless Love*

First Monday in October

Mommie Dearest

My Dinner with Andre

Pennies from Heaven

Prince of the City

Raggedy Man

Ragtime

Reds*

S.O.B.

The Four Seasons*

The French Lieutenant's Woman

Whose Life is it Anyway?

Zoot Suit

Zorro, the Gay Blade

BLOCKBUSTERS

Raiders of the Lost Ark **

Superman II

Bustin' Loose

Caveman

Cheech & Chong's Nice Dreams

Clash of the Titans

Escape From New York

Excalibur

For Your Eyes Only

Fort Apache, The Bronx

History of the World: Part I

Mad Max 2: Road Warrior

Modern Problems

Porky's

Private Lessons

Sharky's Machine

Stripes

Take This Job and Shove It

Taps

Tarzan, The Ape Man

The Cannonball Run

The Night the Lights Went Out in Georgia

Time Bandits

CRITICALLY ACCLAIMED

American Pop

Butterfly

Continental Divide

Dragonslayer

Four Friends

Gregory's Girl

Heartbeeps

Montenegro

Only When I Laugh

Polyester

The Jazz Singer

The Postman Always Rings Twice

Thief

Victory

DOCUMENTARIES

Against Wind and Tide:
A Cuban Odyssey

Brooklyn Bridge

Eight Minutes to Midnight:
A Portrait of Dr. Helen Caldicott

El Salvador: Another Vietnam

Front Line

Genocide

Just Another Missing Kid

Soldier Girls

The Decline of Western Civilization   *Vernon, Florida*

Trances

FOR THE FAMILY & KIDS

Feherlofia - Son of the White Mare   The Great Muppet Caper*

It's Magic, Charlie Brown   The Legend of the Lone Ranger

Revenge of the Mysterons from Mars   The Little Fox

Roar   The Looney Looney Looney
Bugs Bunny Movie

Swan Lake
       The Mystery of the Third Planet

The Fox and the Hound*
       Unico

FOREIGN FILMS

Man of Iron   POL

Mephisto   HUN

Beau-Pere   FR

Blind Chance   POL

BRD Trilogy II: Lola   GER

Christiane F.   GER

Coup de Torchon   FR

Das Boot   GER

Diva   FR

Do You Remember Dolly Bell?   BOS

Faster, Faster   SPA/FR

Gallipoli   AUT

Macumba Sexual   SPA

Make Them Die Slowly   IT

Marianne and Juliane   GER

Muddy River   JPN

No Mercy No Future   GER

Quest for Fire   CAN

The Aviator's Wife   FR

The Boat   GER

The Boat is Full   SWZ

The Burning/Carnage   FR

The Cabbage Soup   FR

Three Brothers   IT

HONORABLE MENTION

A Friend Is a Treasure

Adieu, Galaxy Express 999:
Last Stop Andromeda

Bloody Birthday

Buddy Buddy

Comin' at Ya! 3D

Eyes of a Stranger

Fantasies

Hard Country

Heavy Metal

Knightriders

Looker

Modern Romance

Ms. 45

Rich and Famous

Roadgames

Southern Comfort

Tattoo

The Amateur

The Devil and Max Devlin

The Girl with The Red Hair

The Incredible Shrinking Woman

The Prodigal Son

The Pursuit of DB Cooper

The Woman Next Door

HORROR & CULT

Anthropophagus: The Grim Reaper

Hell Night

Blood Beach

Horrorplanet

Cutter's Way

My Bloody Valentine

Dark Night of the Scarecrow

Neighbors

Deadly Blessing

Night School/Terror Eyes

Don't Go in the Woods

Nighthawks

Enter the Ninja

Nightmare

Eyes of the Needle

Omen III: The Final Conflict*

Eyewitness

Outland

Fear No Evil

Piranha II: The Spawning

Friday the 13th Part II*

Possession

Ghost Story

Scanners*

Halloween 2*

Taxi to the Toilet

The Black Cat	The Pit
The Day of the Triffids	The Professional… All the Marbles
The Evil Dead*	The Strange Case of Dr. Jekyll and Miss Osbourne
The Funhouse	
	The Watcher in the Woods
The Goat	
	True Confessions
The Howling*	
	Wolfen*
The Nesting	
	Yuniko

MADE FOR TV

Brideshead Revisited	Cannibal Ferox
A Long Way Home	East of Eden
A Matter of Life and Death	Jacqueline Bouvier Kennedy
Bill	The People Vs. Jean Harris

THIS MOVIE SUCKS

All Night Long

Paternity

An Eye for An Eye

So Fine

Carbon Copy

The Fan

Condorman

The Hand

Going Ape!

The Prowler

Inchon

Under the Rainbow

On the Right Track

Venom

<u>NOTES</u>

What are your go-to movie snacks?

1980 AWARD SEASON

Coal Miner's Daughter*

Ordinary People   [2]

The Elephant Man*

9 to 5*

Airplane!*

Altered States

American Gigolo

Dressed to Kill*

Fame

Gloria

Heaven's Gate

Inside Movies

Melvin and Howard

Private Benjamin*

Raging Bull*

Resurrection

Somewhere in Time

Stir Crazy*

The Bed Red One

The Blue Lagoon*

The Idolmaker

The Ninth Configuration

The Stunt Man

Urban Cowboy*

BLOCKBUSTERS

Star Wars: Episode V
The Empire Strikes Back **

Flash Gordon

Little Darlings

Any Which Way You Can

Popeye

Bronco Billy

Smokey and the Bandit II

Brubaker

The Blues Brothers

Caddyshack

Cheech & Chong's Next Movie

CRITICALLY ACCLAIMED

Carny

Stardust Memories

Cruising

The Gods Must Be Crazy

Hopscotch

The Long Good Friday

My Bodyguard

The Long Riders

Out of the Blue

Tribute

Personal Problems

Used Cars

DOCUMENTARIES

Agee

The Life and Times of
Rosie the Riveter

The Day After Trinity

The Yellow Star: The Persecution
of the Jews in Europe: 1933-45

FOR THE FAMILY & KIDS

Bon Voyage, Charlie Brown
(and Don't Come Back!!)

The Last Flight of Noah's Ark

The Return of the King:
A Story of the Hobbits

Little Lord Fauntleroy

Never Never Land

The World of Strawberry Shortcake

The King and the Mockingbird

Yogi's First Christmas

FOREIGN FILMS

*Kagemusha:
The Shadow Warrior*   JPN

Bad Timing   UK

Berlin Alexanderplatz   GER

Moscow Does Not Believe
in Tears   USSR

Breaker Morant   AUT

Atlantic City   CAN

Confidence   HUN

Every Man for Himself FR

Loulov FR

My American Uncle FR

Palermo or Wolfsburg GER

Pixote: The Law of the Weakest BRZ

Shogun Assassin JPN

Special Treatment YUG

Teddy Bear POL

The Last Metro FR

The Nest SPA

The Young Master HK

Who Sings Over There SER

Zigeunerweisen JPN

HORROR & CULT

Alligator

Christmas Evil

City of Women

Fade to Black

Forbidden Zone

Friday the 13th *

Motel Hell

Nightmare City

Terror Train

The Falls

The Shining*

MADE FOR TV

The Shadow Box

Playing for Time

A Tale of Two Cities

The Diary of Anne Frank

Oppenheimer

THIS MOVIE SUCKS

A Change of Seasons

The Apple

Can't Stop the Music

The Formula

Honeysuckle Rose

The Island

It's My Turn

The Jazz Singer

Middle Age Crazy

The Man with Bogart's Face

New York Ninja

The Nude Bomb

Saturn 3

Windows

Seems Like Old Times

Xanadu

<u>NOTES</u>

Do you keep movie stubs? Is there a particular one you hold dear?

1979 AWARD SEASON

*All That Jazz**

Breaking Away

Kramer vs. Kramer* **[2]**

*Manhattan**

10*

1941*

A Little Romance

Agatha

Alien*

...And Justice for All*

Apocalypse Now*

Being There

Chapter Two

Hair

Meteor

Norma Rae

Star Trek: The Motion Picture*

Starting Over

The Black Hole*

*The Black Stallion**

The China Syndrome

The Europeans

The Muppet Movie*

The Promise

The Rose

Yanks

BLOCKBUSTERS

Moonraker

Rocky II

Butch and Sundance:
The Early Days

Escape from Alcatraz

Love at First Bite

Penitentiary

The Electric Horseman

The In-Laws

The Jerk

The Main Event

The Wanderers

CRITICALLY ACCLAIMED

Buck Rogers in the 25th Century

Chilly Scenes of Winter

Hanover Street

Hardcore

Heartland

La Luna

Love on the Run

Meatballs

Monty Python's Life of Brian

Over the Edge

Promises in the Dark

Real Life

1979

Scum

The Onion Field

The Great Santini

The Warriors

The Hypothesis
of the Stolen Painting

Time After Time

Wise Blood

DOCUMENTARIES

Best Boy

The Killing Ground

From Mao to Mozart:
Isaac Stern in China

The War at Home

Generation on the Wind

With Babies and Banners:
Story of the Women's Emergency
Brigade

Going the Distance

FOR THE FAMILY & KIDS

C.H.O.M.P.S.

Tale of Tales

Lupin III:
The Castle of Cagliostro

Tarka the Otter

Mountain Family Robinson

Taro the Dragon Boy

The Adventure of Sudsakorn

The North Avenue Irregulars

The Bugs Bunny/Road Runner Movie

Unidentified Flying Oddball

FOREIGN FILMS

Birds of a Feather   FR/IT

Tess   UK

The Tin Drum   FR/GER   **[2]**

Beyond the Darkness   IT

Camera Buff   POL

Coup de Tete   FR

David   GER

Demon Pond   JPN

Don Giovanni   FR/IT

Forget Venice   IT

Last Hurrah for Chivalry   HK

Mad Max   AUS

Mama Turns 100   SPA

My Brilliant Career   AUT

Stalker   USSR

Suhaag   IND

The Fearless Hyena   HK/KOR

The Maids of Wilko   POL

The Man Who Stole the Sun   JPN

The Marriage of Maria Braun   GER

Thirst   AUS   Woyzeck   GER

Vengeance is Mine   JPN   Zulu Dawn   NLD/US

HONORABLE MENTION

All Quiet on the Western Front   North Dallas Forty

Baby Snakes   Rock and Roll High School

Galaxy Express 999   The Champ

Disco Godfather   The Frisco Kid

More American Graffiti   The Shape of Things to Come

HORROR & CULT

Dracula

Killer Nun

Nosferatu the Vampire

Phantasm*

Prophecy

The Amityville Horror*

The Brood

The Legacy

The Visitor

They Eat Scum

Tourist Trap

When a Stranger Calls

Winter Kills

Zombie

MADE FOR TV

Elvis

Roots: The Next Generation

Friendly Fire

Salem's Lot

From Here to Eternity

The Miracle Worker

Goldengirl

RATED X

Caligula*

Memoirs of a French Whore

<u>NOTES</u>

Who would play **You** in the movie of your Life?

1978 AWARD SEASON

Heaven Can Wait*

Midnight Express*

The Deer Hunter*

A Wedding

An Unmarried Woman

California Suite

Coming Home*

Corvette Summer

Days of Heaven

Foul Play*

Ice Castles

Interiors

Invasion of the Body Snatchers*

King of the Gypsies

Magic

Movie Movie

Same Time, Next Year

Slow Dancing in the Big City

Stevie

The Boys from Brazil

The Brink's Job

The Buddy Holly Story

The Children of Sanchez

The Wiz*

Uncle Joe Shannon

Who is Killing the Great Chefs of Europe?

BLOCKBUSTERS

Grease **	Hooper
Superman **	House Calls
Cheech & Chong Up in Smoke	National Lampoon's Animal House
Convoy	Revenge of the Pink Panther
Every Which Way but Loose	Sgt. Pepper's Lonely Hearts Club Band
F.I.S.T.	The One and Only
Goin' South	The Other Side of the Mountain Part II

CRITICALLY ACCLAIMED

American Hot Wax	Force 10 from Navarone
Big Wednesday	Girlfriends
Comes a Horseman	Moment by Moment
Death on the Nile	Paradise Alley

1978

Straight Time

Thank God, It's Friday

The Big Fix

The Driver

The Greek Tycoon

<u>DOCUMENTARIES</u>

Scared Straight

The Tree of Wooden Clogs

Always for Pleasure

Gates of Heaven

Killer of Sheep

Koko: A Talking Gorilla

Mysterious Castles of Clay

Raoni

The Lovers Wind

FOR THE FAMILY & KIDS

Blue Fin

The Cat from Outer Space

Candleshoe

The Further Adventures of
the Wilderness Family

Casey's Shadow

The Lord of the Rings

Hot Lead and Cold Feet

The Magic of Lassie

International Velvet

The Water Babies

Return From Witch Mountain

FOREIGN FILMS

Autumn Sonata   SWE

Crippled Avengers   HK

Get Out Your
Handkerchiefs   FR

Double Suicide of Sonezaki   JPN

A Dream of Passion   GRC

Drunken Master   HK

A Simple Story   FR

Empire of Passion   JPN

BRD Trilogy I:
The Marriage of Maria Braun   GER

Going All the Way   ISR

Half a Loaf of Kung Fu   TAI/HK

Hungarians   HUN

La Cage Aux Folles   FR

Lemon Popsicle   IRL/GER

Lillie   BBC

Shaolin Master Killer:
The 36th Chamber of Shaolin   HK

Spiritual Kung Fu   HK/TAI

The Chant of Jimmie Blacksmith
AUT

The Demon   JPN

The Glass Cell   GER

HONORABLE MENTION

Blue Collar

Brass Target

Caravans

Five Deadly Venoms

Gray Lady Down

I Wanna Hold Your Hand

Nunzio

Our Winning Season

Pretty Baby

Skateboard

The Bad News Bears Go to Japan

The End

HORROR & CULT

Damien: Omen II*	*Jubilee*
Dawn of the Dead*	Piranha*
Eyes of Laura Mars*	Terror
Faces of Death	The Fury*
Halloween*	The Toolbox Murders
I Spit on Your Grave	They Call Her… Cleopatra Wong
Jaws 2*	*Watership Down*
Jennifer	

MADE FOR TV

Holocaust	The Rutles: All You Need is Cash

RATED X

Debbie Does Dallas	Tatuaje

THIS MOVIE SUCKS

The Star Wars Holiday Special   The Swarm

<u>NOTES</u>

What's your first memory of watching a movie? How old were you?

1977 AWARD SEASON

Annie Hall* **[3]**

Julia*

The Goodbye Girl

The Turning Point*

A Little Night Music

Bobby Deerfield

Close Encounters of the Third Kind*

Equus

High Anxiety*

I Never Promised You a
Rose Garden

Last Chants for a Slow Dance

Looking for Mr. Goodbar*

MacArthur

New York, New York

Pete's Dragon

Pumping Iron

Saturday Night Fever*

Sorcerer

The Deep*

The Duelists

The Late Show

You Light Up My Life

BLOCKBUSTERS

Star Wars: Episode IV
A New Hope **

Semi-Tough

A Bridge Too Far

Slap Shot

Black Sunday

Smokey and the Bandit

Heroes

The Gauntlet

The Spy Who Loved Me

Oh, God!

CRITICALLY ACCLAIMED

3 Women

Jabberwocky

A Piece of the Action

Joseph Andrews

Alambrista!

March or Die

Citizens Band

Roseland

Fraternity Row

The Message

Islands in the Stream

Twilight's Last Gleaming

DOCUMENTARIES

Who Are the DeBolts? And
Where Did They Get 19 Kids?

La Soufrière –
Waiting for an Inevitable Disaster

High Grass Circus

The Children of Theatre Street

Homage to Chagall:
The Colours of Love

FOR THE FAMILY & KIDS

Blue Fire Lady

Return to Boggy Creek

Candleshoe

Sinbad and the Eye of the Tiger

Dot and the Kangaroo

The Bad News Bears in
Breaking Training*

For the Love of Benji

The Billion Dollar Hobo

Freaky Friday*

The Glitterball

Gulliver's Travels

The Hobbit

Herbie Goes to Monte Carlo*

The Many Adventures of
Winnie the Pooh

Raggedy Ann & Andy:
A Musical Adventure

The Mouse and His Child

The Rescuers

The Prince and the Pauper

Wombling Free

FOREIGN FILMS

A Special Day   IT

Iphigenia   GRC

Madame Rosa   FR

Man of Marble   POL

Padre Padrone   IT

Mighty Peking Man   HK

A Little Night Music
US/AUT/GER

One Sings, The Other Doesn't   FR

Aina   PAK

Operation Thunderbolt   ISR

Raise Ravens   SPA

Baxter, Vera Baxter   FR

Shaolin Invincibles   TAI

Ceddo   FR/SEN

Sleeping Dogs   NZL

Chinatown Kid   HK

Soldier of Orange   NLD

El Pez Que Fuma   VEN

That Obscure Object of Desire   FR

Executioners from Shaolin   HK

The American Friend   GER

The Ascent   USSR

Viva Italia!   IT

The Yellow Handkerchief   JPN

White Bim Black Ear   USSR

HORROR & CULT

Alucarda

Prey

Death Bed: The Bed That Eats

Rolling Thunder

Demon Seed

Satan's Cheerleaders

Desperate Living

Shock

Eraserhead

Shock Waves

Exorcist II: The Heretic*

Stroszek

House   JPN

Suspiria

Martin

The Hills Have Eyes

Orca

The Last Wave

MADE FOR TV

Just a Little Inconvenience

Something for Joey

Mary White

The Gathering

Raid on Entebbe

Washington: Behind Closed Doors

Roots

<u>NOTES</u>

Who is your favorite movie character?

1976 AWARD SEASON

A Star Is Born*

Rocky   [2]

1900

All the President's Men*

Bound for Glory

Bugsy Malone

Carrie

Family Plot

Fellini's Casanova

King Kong*

Logan's Run

Network

Obsession

Silent Movie

Taxi Driver

The Duchess and the Dirtwater Fox

The Incredible Sarah

The Passover Plot

The Pink Panther Strikes Again

The Ritz

The Sailor Who Fell From Grace with the Sea

The Seven-Per-Cent Solution

Two-Minute Warning

Voyage of the Damned

1976

BLOCKBUSTERS

Car Wash

Silver Streak

In Search of Noah's Ark

Sparkle

Midway

The Enforcer

CRITICALLY ACCLAIMED

Assault on Precinct 13

The Killing of a Chinese Bookie

Half a House

The Last Tycoon

Mikey and Nicky

The Man Who Fell to Earth

The Front

The Outlaw Josey Wales

DOCUMENTARIES

Alters of the World

Harlan County, USA

Youthquake!

High Grass Circus

Hollywood on Trial

People of the Wind

That's Entertainment Part II

Volcano: An Inquiry into the Life and Death of Malcolm Lowry

FOR THE FAMILY & KIDS

Across the Great Divide

Escape from the Dark

Gus

Let the Balloon Go

No Deposit, No Return

Storm Boy

The Bad News Bears

The Shaggy D.A.

The Slipper and the Rose: The Story of Cinderella

The Smurfs and the Magic Flute

The Twelve Tasks of Asterix

Treasure of Matecumbe

FOREIGN FILMS

Face to Face   SWE

In the Realm of the Senses FR/JPN

An Elephant Can Be Extremely
Deceptive   FR

Letters From Marusia   MEX

Black and White in Color
IVO/FR/GER/SWZ

Mr. Klein   FR

Canoa: A Shameful Memory   MEX

Pocket Money   FR

Cria Cuervos…   SPA

The Mistress   SPA

Dona Flor and
Her Two Husbands   BRZ

*The Road Trilogy:
Kings of the Road*   GER

Fill 'er Up with Super   FR

Watcher in the Attic   JPN

HORROR & CULT

Allegro Non Troppo

Satan's Slave

Bloodsucking Freaks

Shaolin Temple

Dogs (Killerhunde)

The Omen*

God Told Me To

The Tenant

House on Straw Hill

MADE FOR TV

Captains and the Kings

Helter Skelter

Dawn: Portrait of a Teenage
Runaway

I Want to Keep My Baby

Rich Man, Poor Man

Eleanor and Franklin

Sybil

Francis Gary Powers: The True
Story of the U2 Spy Incident

The Lindbergh Kidnapping Case

RATED X

Salon Kitty

The Opening of Misty Beethoven

Sebastiane

Up!

Sensational Janine

THIS MOVIE SUCKS

The Angel Was a Devil

<u>NOTES</u>

Favorite movie genre? Favorite film of that genre?

1975 AWARD SEASON & BLOCKBUSTERS

Jaws

One Flew Over the
Cuckoo's Nest   [3]

The Sunshine Boys

Barry Lyndon

Dog Day Afternoon

Funny Lady

Hedda

Jacqueline Susann's
Once is Not Enough

Lucky Lady

Mahogany

Nashville

Paper Tiger

Shampoo

The Day of the Locust

The Fortune

The Hiding Place

The Man in the Glass Booth

The Man Who Would Be King

The Master Gunfighter

The Other Side of the Mountain

The Return of the Pink Panther

The Wind and the Lion

Three Days of the Condor

Tommy

Whiffs

DOCUMENTARIES

The Man Who Skied
Down Everest

Brother, Can You Spare a Dime?

Fighting for Our Lives

Grey Gardens

Hearts and Minds

The California Reich

The Gentleman Tramp

The Incredible Machine

The Other Half of the Sky:
A China Memoir

FOR THE FAMILY & KIDS

Against a Crooked Sky

Be My Valentine, Charlie Brown

Escape to Witch Mountain

One of Our Dinosaurs is Missing

Ride a Wild Pony

The Adventures
of the Wilderness Family

The Apple Dumpling Gang*

The Pinchcliffe Grand Prix

The Strongest Man in the World

Tubby the Tuba

1975

FOREIGN FILMS

Chronicle of the
Years of Fire   ALG

Dersu Uzala   USSR

Lies My Father Told
Me   CAN

Cousin Cousine   FR

Deep Red   IT

Fox and His Friends   GER

India Song   FR

*Jeanne Dielman, 23, Quai du
Commerce, 1080 Bruxelles*   FR

Maîtresse   FR

Manila in the Claws of Light   PHL

My Friends   IT

Nights and Days   POL

Seven Beauties   IT

Sholay   IND

Special Section   FR

The Lost Honour of Katharina Blum,
or How Violence Develops and
Where It Can Lead   GER

The Magic Flute   SWE

The Mirror   USSR

The Promised Land   POL

*The Road Trilogy:
The Wrong Move*   GER

The Shiranui Sea   JPN

The Wall   IND

HONORABLE MENTION

Aaron Loves Angela

Mandingo

Bucktown

Not a Pretty Picture

Cooley High

Rollerball

Cornbread, Earl and Me

Sheba Baby

Friday Foster

The Black Gestapo

Let's Do It Again

Welcome Home, Brother Charles

HORROR & CULT

A Boy and His Dog

Salò, or the 120 Days of Sodom

Coonskin

Shanks

Death Race 2000

Shivers

Hugo the Hippo

Terror of Mechagodzilla

Lisztomania

Thundercrack!

Race with the Devil

Trip With the Teacher

MADE FOR TV

The Legend of Lizzie Borden

Trilogy of Terror

RATED X

Inserts

The Story of O

The Image

THIS MOVIE SUCKS

At Long Last Love

Snuff

Emmanuelle II

<u>NOTES</u>

What's the last memorable movie night with your family? With whom?

1974 AWARD SEASON

Alice Doesn't Live
Here Anymore

Chinatown

The Godfather Part II*

The Longest Yard*

The Conversation

99 and 44/100% Dead

A Woman Under the Influence

Ali: Fear Eats the Soul

Badlands

Benji

Bring Me the Head of Alfredo Garcia

Celine and Julie Go Boating

Claudine

Earthquake*

Female Trouble

Harry and Tonto

Lenny

Mame

The Front Page

The Great Gatsby

The Little Prince

The Taking of Pelham 123

The Three Musketeers

Willie Dynamite

BLOCKBUSTERS

The Towering Inferno **

The Life and Times of
Grizzly Adams

Airport 1975

The Trial of Billy Jack

Blazing Saddles

Young Frankenstein

Murder on the Orient Express

CRITICALLY ACCLAIMED

Freebie and the Bear

That's Entertainment

Foxy Brown

Uptown Saturday Night

DOCUMENTARIES

Animals Are Beautiful People

Birds Do It, Bees Do It

Hearts and Minds

Cree Hunters of Mistassini

A Poem is a Naked Person

*General Idi Amin Dada:
A Self Portrait*

Always A New Beginning

I Am a Dancer

Antonia: A Portrait of the Woman

James

The Wild and the Brace

The 81st Blow

UFOs: Past Present and Future

The Challenge:
A Tribute to Modern Art

FOR THE FAMILY & KIDS

Castaway Cowboy

The Golden Fortress

Herbie Rides Again*

The Golden Voyage of Sinbad

Jack and the Beanstalk

The Island at the Top of the World

Journey Back to Oz

Where the Lilies Bloom

Professor Popper's Problem

Where the Red Fern Grows

Swallows and Amazons

FOREIGN FILMS

Lacombe, Lucien   FR

And Now My Love   FR

Arabian Nights   IT

Final Episode   JPN

Five Shaolin Masters   HK/TAI

Going Places   FR

Lone Wolf and Cub:
White Heaven in Hell   JPN

Parade   FR

Sandakan No. 8   JPN

Scent of a Woman   IT

Sweet Movie   YUG

The Apprenticeship of
Duddy Kravitz   CAN

The Deer   IRN

The Deluge   POL

The Enigma of Kaspar Hauser   GER

The Night Porter   IT

The Phantom of Liberty   FR

The Road Trilogy: Alice in the Cities
GER

The Truce   ARG

Till Marriage Do Us Part   IT

Violent Streets   JPN

HONORABLE MENTION

Black Belt Jones

Black Samson

Boss Nigger

Sins of the Flesh

Three the Hard Way

Truck Turner

HORROR & CULT

Act of Vengeance

Beyond the Door

Cockfighter

Dark Star

Impulse

Lady Snowblood:
Love Song of Vengeance

Lucifer Rising

Messiah of Evil

Phantom of the Paradise

Shriek of the Mutilated

Space is the Place

Steppenwolf

The Arena

The Parallax View

The Texas Chainsaw Massacre*

Zardoz

MADE FOR TV

Bad Ronald

Planet Earth

Born Innocent

The Missiles of October

Martha

Winter Kill

RATED X

Emmanuelle

The 9 Lives of Fritz the Cat

Lorna the Exorcist

<u>NOTES</u>

What is one thing you look for in a movie?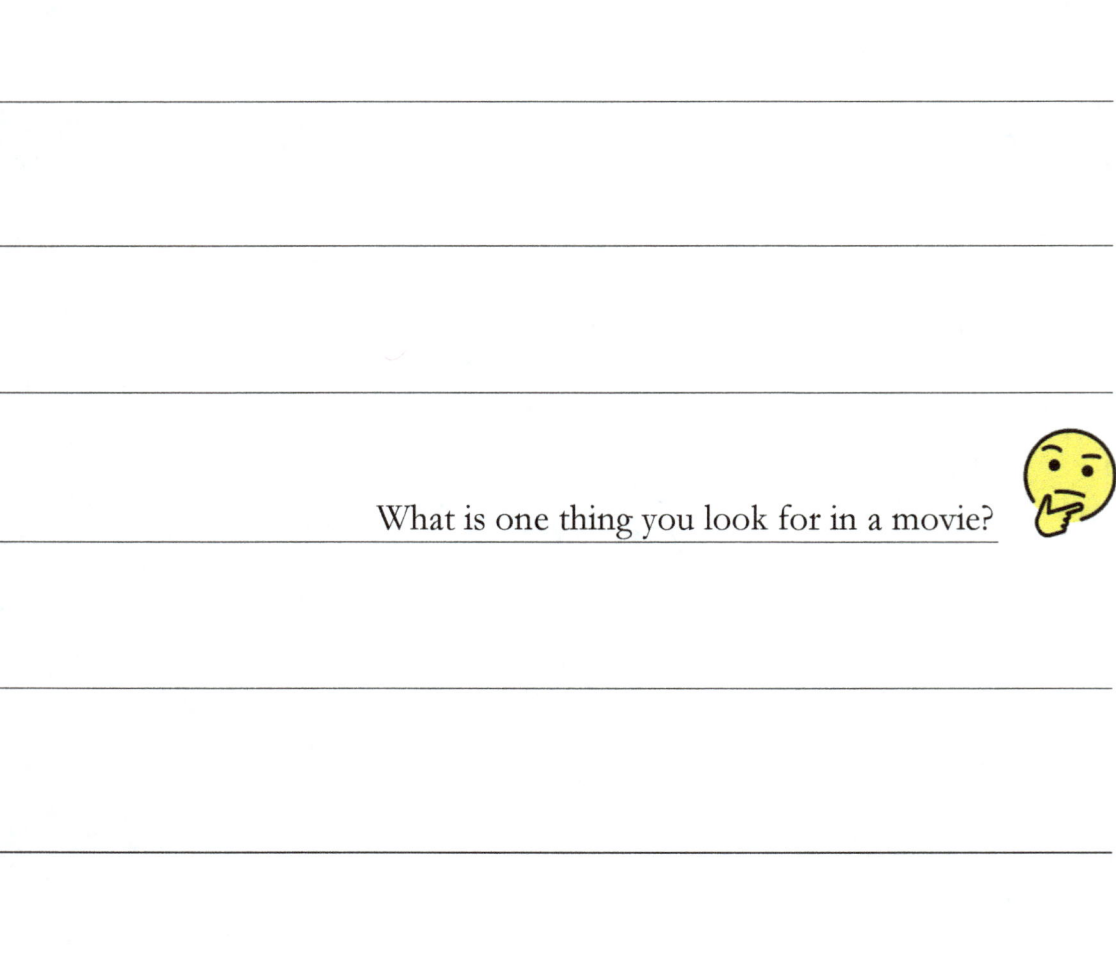

1973 AWARD SEASON

American Graffiti*

Scarecrow

The Exorcist*

The Sting*

A Touch of Class

Brother Sun, Sister Moon

Cinderella Liberty

Don't Look Now

Jesus Christ Superstar

Jonathan Livingston Seagull

Last Tango in Paris*

Live and Let Die*

Ludwig

O Lucky Man!

Paper Moon

Save the Tiger

Serpico

Summer Wishes, Winter Dreams

The Day of the Jackal

The Last Detail

The Paper Chase

The Way We Were*

Tom Sawyer

BLOCKBUSTERS

Coffy

Cries and Whispers

Enter the Dragon

High Plains Drifter

Magnum Force

Papillon

Robin Hood

Soylent Green

CRITICALLY ACCLAIMED

40 Carats

A Delicate Balance

Ash Wednesday

Badlands

Breezy

Electra Glide in Blue

Mean Streets

Sisters

Pat Garrett and Billy the Kid

The Long Goodbye

The Three Musketeers

Westworld

DOCUMENTARIES

The Great American Cowboy

Love

Battle of Berlin

The Autobiography of
Miss Jane Pittman

Black Caesar

The Movies That Made Us

Black Mama White Mama

The Second Gun

F for Fake

The Spook Who Sat by The Door

Hotel Monterey

Visions of Eight

Journey to the Outer Limits

Wattstax

FOR THE FAMILY & KIDS

A Charlie Brown Thanksgiving

From the Mixed-Up Files
of Mrs. Basil E. Frankweiler

Charley and the Angel

One Little Indian

Charlotte's Web

The World's Greatest Athlete

Digby the Biggest Dog in the World

Three Wishes for Cinderella

Fantastic Planet

FOREIGN FILMS

Amarcord   IT

Day for Night   FR   **[2]**

Scenes from a Marriage   SWE

The Pedestrian   GER

A River Called Titas   IND/BAN

Battles Without Honour
and Humanity   JPN

Bobby   IND

Distant Thunder   IND

Kazablan   ISR

Lady Snowblood   JPN

L'Invitation   SWZ

Lone Wolf and Cub   JPN
V. Baby Cart in the Land of Demons

Malicious   IT

The Hireling   UK

The House of 72 Tenants   HK

The House of Chebouche St   ISR

The Mad Adventures of
Rabbi Jacob   FR

The Mother and the Whore   FR

The Spirit of the Beehive   SPA

Touki Bouki   SEN

Turkish Delight   NLD

World on a Wire   GER

Zatoichi's Conspiracy   JPN

HONORABLE MENTION

Cleopatra Jones	Hell Up in Harlem
Detroit 9000	Jeremy
Dillinger	Oklahoma Crude
Five on the Black Hand Side	Super Fly TNT
Ganja & Hess	The Harder They Come
Heavy Traffic	The Mack

HORROR & CULT

Alabama's Ghost	Hollywood 90028
Baby Yaga, Devil Witch	I Will Walk Like a Crazy Horse
Battle for The Planet of the Apes	The Baby
Belladonna of Sadness	The Day of the Dolphin
Female Prisoner Scorpion: Beast Stable	The Death Wheelers
	The Holy Mountain
Flesh for Frankenstein	

The Hourglass Sanatorium

Themroc

The Wicker Man

MADE FOR TV

Don't Be Afraid of the Dark

The Night Strangler

RATED X

Anita: Swedish Nymphet

Immoral Tales

Early Awakening Report

The Blue Knight

Female Vampire

The Devil in Miss Jones*

Hangover

The Loreley's Grasp

<u>NOTES</u>

Favorite drama?

1972 AWARD SEASON

Cabaret* **[2]**

The Godfather **[2]**

1776

Aguirre, the Wrath of God

Avanti!

Ben

Buck and the Preacher

Butterflies Are Free

Deliverance*

Frenzy

Limelight

Man of La Mancha

Pete n Tillie

Sleuth

Sounder

The Candidate

The Hot Rock

The King of Marvin Gardens

The Life and Times of
Judge Roy Bean

The Little Ark

The Poseidon Adventure*

The Stepmother

Travels with My Aunt

BLOCKBUSTERS

Everything You Always
Wanted to Know About Sex
*But Were Afraid to Ask

Superfly

The Getaway

Jeremiah Johnson

What's Up, Doc?

Lady Sings the Blues

DOCUMENTARIES

Elvis on Tour

Malcolm X

Marjoe

The RA Expeditions

The Silent Revolution

Ape and Superape

FOR THE FAMILY & KIDS

Hide and Seek

Oliver and the Artful Dodger

Justin Morgan Had a Horse

Santa and the Ice Cream Bunny

Napoleon and Samantha

Snoopy, Come Home

Now You See Him, Now You Don't

Snowball Express

The Biscuit Eater

The Amazing Mr. Blunden

Veronica

FOREIGN FILMS

The Emigrants   SWE

I Love You Rosa   ISR

The Mattei Affair   IT

Lone Wolf and Cub Series   JPN
I. Sword of Vengeance
II. Baby Cart at the River Styx

The New Land   SWE

III. Baby Cart to Hades
IV. Baby Cart in Peril

Young Winston   UK

A Day in the Death of Joe Egg   UK

Mirage   PER

Alfredo, Alfredo   IT

My Dearest Senorita   SPA

Picture of the Old World   SVN

Cats Play   HUN

Cries and Whispers   SWE

Red Psalm   HUN

Downpour   IRN

Roma   IT

Eight Hours Don't Make a Day   GER

Six Moral Tales series
VI. Love in the Afternoon   FR

Solaris   USSR

State of Siege   FR

The Bitter Tears of
Petra Von Kant   GER

The Dawns Here Are Quiet   USSR

*The Discreet Charm of
the Bourgeoisie*   FR

The Headless Horseman
USSR/CUB

The Merchant of Four Seasons   GER

Tout Va Bien   FR/IT

Zatoichi at Large

Zatoichi in Desperation   JPN

HONORABLE MENTION

Across 110th Street

Fat City

Silent Running

The Man

Tomorrow

Trick Baby

Ulzana's Raid

HORROR & CULT

A Bay of Blood

Pink Flamingos

Black Gunn

The Blood Splattered Bride

Cool Breeze

The Boxer from Shantung

Don't Torture a Duckling

The Howl

Female Prisoner Scorpion:
Jailhouse 41

The Last House on the Left

The Possession of Joel Delaney

Five Fingers of Death

The Ruling Class

Greaser's Palace

Trouble Man

MADE FOR TV

A War of Children

That Certain Summer

Blaise Pascal

The Glass House

Footsteps

The Night Stalker

Gargoyles

<u>RATED X</u>

Beyond the Green Door*

Deep Throat*

Fritz the Cat

The Canterbury Tales

The Gore Gore Girls

<u>NOTES</u>

What's the most heartwarming movie moment you've ever witnessed?

1971 AWARD SEASON

Fiddler on the Roof*

The French Connection [2]

A Clockwork Orange*

A New Leaf

Carnal Knowledge*

Get Carter

Harold and Maude

Klute

Kotch

MacBeth

Mary, Queen of Scots

McCabe & Mrs. Miller

Nicholas and Alexandra

Play Misty for Me

Plaza Suite

Shaft

Straw Dogs

Summer of '42*

Sweet Sweetback's Baad Asssss Song

The Boy Friend

The Last Picture Show*

Willy Wonka
and the Chocolate Factory*

BLOCKBUSTERS

Diamonds Are Forever

The Grissom Gang

Billy Jack

The Hired Hand

Cisco Pike

The Last Movie

Dirty Harry

They Might Be Giants

The Andromeda Strain

THX 1138

The Beguiled

Willard

CRITICALLY ACCLAIMED

A Safe Place

The African Elephant

Bananas

The Raging Moon

Drive, He Said

The Seven Minutes

Friends

Two-Lane Blacktop

Red Sky at Morning

Vanishing Point

Star Spangled Girl

Wanda

Such Good Friends

DOCUMENTARIES

Alaska Wilderness Lake	Say Goodbye
Death of a Legend	The Hellstrom Chronicle
Eat the Document	Town Bloody Hall
On Any Sunday	Walls of Fire

FOR THE FAMILY & KIDS

$1,000,000 Duck	Scandalous John
A Christmas Carol	Tales of Beatrix Potter
Bedknobs and Broomsticks	The Barefoot Executive
Black Beauty	The Million Dollar Duck
Flight of the Doves	The Point!
Here Comes Peter Cottontail	

FOREIGN FILMS

Sunday Bloody Sunday   UK

The Go-Between   UK

The Policeman   ISR

The Working Class Goes to Heaven   IT

10 Rillington Place   UK

A Touch of Zen   CH

Death in Venice   IT

Evdokia   GRC

Just Before Nightfall   FR

La Moglie Piu Bella   IT

Murmur of the Heart   FR

My Uncle Antoine   CAN

The Decameron   IT

The Emigrants   SWE

The Long Farewell   USSR

Throw Away Your Books, Rally in the Streets   JPN

To Die of Love   FR

Traffic   IT/FR

Walkabout   UK/AUT

WR: Mysteries of the Organism YUG/GER

Zatoichi Meets the One-Armed Swordsman   JPN

HORROR & CULT

200 Motels

Countess Dracula

Fata Morgana

Goodbye Uncle Tom

Johnny Got His Gun

Let's Scare Jessica to Death

Long Live Death

Malpertius

The Abominable Dr. Phibes

The Cat O'Nine Tails

The Devils

The Omega Man*

The Telephone Book

The Velvet Vampire

Up Your Legs Forever

Wake in Fright

<u>MADE FOR TV</u>

Brian's Song

Duel

The Last Child

The Snow Goose

The Waltons: The Homecoming
A Christmas Story

<u>THIS MOVIE SUCKS</u>

Zaat

<u>NOTES</u>

Worst movie you've ever seen? Ever walk out of a movie?

1970 AWARD SEASON

Love Story

M*A*S*H*

Patton*

Airport

Beyond the Valley of the Dolls

Catch-22*

Darling Lili

Diary of a Mad Housewife

Five Easy Pieces

Gimme Shelter

I Never Sang for My Father

Little Big Man*

Lovers and Other Strangers

Performance

Ryan's Daughter*

Scrooge

The Bird with the Crystal Plumage

The Honeymoon Killers

The Owl and the Pussycat*

The Private Life of Sherlock Holmes

Tora! Tora! Tora!*

Wanda

Zabriskie Point

CRITICALLY ACCLAIMED

A Man Called Horse

Brewster McCloud

Cotton Comes to Harlem

Equinox

House of Dark Shadows

Husbands

Joe

Kelly's Heroes

Let It Be

Myra Breckinridge

Rio Lobo

Soldier Blue

The Ballad of Cable Hogue

The Boys in the Band

The Tribe

There's a Girl in My Soup

They Call Me Mister Tibbs

They Call Me Trinity

Too Late the Hero

Two Mules for Sister Sara

Watermelon Man

DOCUMENTARIES

Woodstock:
3 Days of Peace & Music*

King: A Filmed Record
Montgomery to Memphis

Before the Mountain Was Moved

Other Voices

Chariots of the Gods

Prologue

Jack Johnson

Sad Song of Yellow Skin

FOR THE FAMILY & KIDS

Aladdin and His Magic Lamp

Santa and the Three Bears

King of the Grizzlies

The Aristocats

Pippi in the South Seas

The Phantom Tollbooth

Pippi on the Run

The Railway Children

Pufnstuf

The Wild Country

FOREIGN FILMS

Investigation of a Citizen Above Suspicion   IT

Rider on the Rain   FR

Baol   GER

Bed and Board   FR

Borsalino   IT

Cromwell   UK

Dodes'ka-den   JPN

Eros + Massacre   JPN

First Love   SWZ

Hoa-Binh   FR

Jibon Theke Neya   BAN

One Day in the Life of Ivan Denisovich   NOR

Peace in the Fields   BEL

Six Moral Tales series   FR
V. Claire's Knee

Soleil O   FR/MRT

Tchaikovsky   USSR

The Confession   FR

The Conformist   IT

The Customer of the Off-Season FR/ISR

The Garden of the Finzi Continis IT/GER

Tristana   SPA

Zatoichi Goes to the Fire Festiva
Zatoichi Meets Yojimbo   JPN

1970

HONORABLE MENTION

Beneath the Planet of the Apes

The Baby Maker

Bloody Mama

The Ear

Chisum

The Magic Christian

Cool It Carol

The Spider's Stratagem

One Song a Day Takes
Mischief Away

The Twelve Chairs

HORROR & CULT

And Soon the Darkness

Eyes Do Not Want to Close
at All Times

Berlin Horse

Multiple Maniacs

Don Juan

Daughters of Darkness

Eden and After

The Wizard of Gore

El Topo

Valerie and Her Week of Wonders

Even Dwarfs Started Small

Zorns Lemma

<u>NOTES</u>

What bad movie do you love? Any guilty pleasures you secretly enjoy?

1969 AWARD SEASON

Anne of the Thousand Days

*Midnight Cowboy** **[2]**

The Secret of Santa Vittoria

Alice's Restaurant

Cactus Flower*

*Easy Rider**

Gaily, Gaily

Goodbye, Columbus*

Hello, Dolly!*

Marooned

Medium Cool

Model Shop

Oh! What a Loving War

Paint Your Wagon*

Take the Money and Run

The Arrangement

The Italian Job

The Learning Tree

The Prime of Miss Jean Brodie

They Shoot Horses, Don't They?

True Grit*

BLOCKBUSTERS

Butch Cassidy and
the Sundance Kid

On Her Majesty's Secret Service

The Wild Bunch

Bob & Carol & Ted & Alice

CRITICALLY ACCLAIMED

Change of Habit

Silent Night, Lonely Night

Downhill Racer

Tell Them Willie Boy is Here

Generation

The Damned

Hail Hero!

The Happy Ending

If It's Tuesday
This Must Be Belgium

The Reivers

The Sterile Cuckoo

John and Mary

Where It's At

Papi

DOCUMENTARIES

Arthur Rubenstein: The Love of Life

The Sorrow and the Pity

Before the Mountain Was Moved

The Wolf Men

The Olympics in Mexico

FOR THE FAMILY & KIDS

A Boy Named Charlie Brown

Pippi Longstocking

Captain Nemo
and the Underwater City

Rascal

Run Wild, Run Free

Frosty the Snowman

The Adventures of Goopy and Bagha

Godzilla's Revenge

The Computer Wore Tennis Shoes

Kes

The Wonderful World
of Puss 'n Boots

My Side of the Mountain

Pippi Goes on Board

Tintin and the Temple of the Sun

1969

FOREIGN FILMS

Z   FR/DZA

Ådalen 31   SWE

Battle of Neretva YUG

Blaumilch Canal   ISR

Fellini Satyricon   IT/FR

Funeral Parade of Roses   JPN

Jack and Jill: A Postscript   AUS

Jackal of Nahueltoro   CHL

Kevade   EST

La Piscine   FR

Rani Radovi   YUG

Red Peony Gambler series
II. 2nd Generation Ceremony
III. The Flower Cards Game   JPN

Satyricon   IT

Six Moral Tales series   FR
IV. My Night with Maud

The Big Dig   ISR

The Boys of Paul Street   HUN

The Brothers Karamazov   USSR

The Cow   IRN

The Night of Counting the Years
EGY

The Red Tent   IT/USSR

The Sorrow and the Pity
FR/SWZ/GER

Women in Love   UK

HONORABLE MENTION

Blind Beast   JPN

Boy   JPN

Chivalrous Geisha   JPN

Dillinger is Dead

Double Suicide   JPN

Goyokin   JPN

Have Sword, Will Travel   HK

Help, Help, the Globolinks!

Hitokiri   JPN

Jigokuhen   JPN

Me, Natalie

Red Lion   JPN

Return of the One-Armed
Swordsman   HK

Samurai Banners

The Cremator   CAE

The Milky Way

Trapped, the Crimson Bat!   JPN

Violent Virgin   JPN

Watch Out, Crimson Bat   JPN

HORROR & CULT

Alice in Acidland

The Girl on a Motorcycle

Horrors of Malformed Men

The Haunted Castle

Night of the Bloody Apes

Witchfinder General

The Castle of Fu Manchu

RATED X

De Sade

The Secret Sex Lives of
Romeo and Juliet

The Laughing Woman

<u>NOTES</u>

What's one word or phrase to describe your movie taste?

1968 AWARD SEASON

Oliver!*   [2]

The Lion in Winter

Buona Sera, Mrs. Campbell

Charly

Faces

Finian's Rainbow*

For Love of Ivy

Hot Millions

Ice Station Zebra

Isadora

Karkatoa, East of Java

Once Upon a Time in the West

Rachel, Rachel

*Romeo and Juliet**

Rosemary's Baby*

Star!

The Fixer

The Heart Is a Lonely Hunter

The Odd Couple*

The Producers

The Scalphunters

The Shoes of the Fisherman

The Subject Was Roses

Wild in the Streets

Yours, Mine and Ours*

BLOCKBUSTERS

| 2001: A Space Odyssey ** |

Funny Girl **

Bandolero!

Barbarella: Queen of the Galaxy

Blackbeard's Ghost

Bullitt

Charlie Bubbles

Chitty Chitty Bang Bang

Coogan's Bluff

Hang 'em High

Night of the Living Dead

Planet of the Apes

Shalako

Speedway

The Ambushers

The Devil's Brigade

The Fox

The Green Berets

The Sweet Ride

The Thomas Crown Affair

Twisted Nerve

Where Were You When the Lights Went Out?

With Six You Get Eggroll

1968

CRITICALLY ACCLAIMED

Danger: Diabolik

Pretty Poison

High School

Targets

Paper Lion

DOCUMENTARIES

Journey Into Self

Symbiopsychotaxiplasm: Take One

A Few Notes on Our Food Problem

The Legendary Champions

In The Year of the Pig

The Queen

Salesman

FOR THE FAMILY & KIDS

Asterix and Cleopatra

The Great Adventure of Horus,
Prince of the Sun

Heidi

The Horse in the Gray Flannel Suit

Never a Dull Moment

The Love Bug

Robby

The One and Only, Genuine,
Original Family Band

Thunderbird 6

The World of Hans Christian
Andersen

FOREIGN FILMS

If... UK

Red Peony Gambler   JPN

Death By Hanging JPN

Retaliation JPN

Destroy All Monsters JPN

Samaritan Zatoichi JPN

Girls in the Sun   GRC

Shame SWE

Kill! JPN

Stolen Kisses   FR

Lucia CUB

The Bofors Gun   UK

Mayerling   UK

The Bride Wore Black   FR

Memories of Underdevelopment CUB

The Color of Pomegranates USSR

Naked Childhood FR

The Girl with the Pistol   IT

Petulia   UK

The Immortal Story FR

The Land of Many Perfumes   HK   Yellow Submarine   UK

The Red Light Bandit   BRZ   *Zatoichi and the Fugitives*   JPN

The Reenactment   ROM

HORROR & CULT

Andy Warhol's Flesh   Skidoo

Candy   Snake Woman's Curse

Death Laid an Egg   *Teorema*

Flesh   The Boston Strangler

Goke, Body Snatcher from Hell   The Blood of Fu Manchu

Head!   The Garden

Hour of the Wolf   The Living Skeleton

Indecent Desires   The Snake Girl and
                                       The Silver Haired Witch

Kuroneko: A Black Cat in
a Bamboo Grove   JPN   The Snow Woman

1968

The Swimmer

RATED X

Inga

The Killing of Sister George

Succubus

Vixen

THIS MOVIE SUCKS

A Place for Lovers

They Saved Hitler's Brain

<u>NOTES</u>

Who is your favorite actor? Why?

1967 AWARD SEASON

In the Heat of the Night   **[2]**

The Graduate *   **[2]**

Banning

Barefoot in the Park*

Beach Red

Bonnie and Clyde*

Camelot*

Cool Hand Luke

Doctor Dolittle*

Far from the Madding Crowd

Guess Who's Coming to Dinner*

In Cold Blood

The Dirty Dozen*

The Happiest Millionaire

The Taming of the Shrew*

The Whisperers

Thoroughly Modern Millie*

To Sir, With Love

Tobruk

Ulysses

Valley of the Dolls *

Wait Until Dark

Woman Times Seven

194

BLOCKBUSTERS

A Fistful of Dollars

Caprice

Casino Royale

Divorce American Style

Easy Come, Easy Go

El Dorado

For a Few Dollars More

Hombre

How to Succeed in Business Without Really Trying

In Like Flint

The Born Losers

The Comedians

The War Wagon

You Only Live Twice

CRITICALLY ACCLAIMED

A Bullet for The General

Point Blank

Requiescat

The Producers

The Trip

DOCUMENTARIES

The Anderson Platoon

Harvest

Don't Look Back

Monterey Pop
With the Complete Festival

Festival

Young Americans

FOR THE FAMILY & KIDS

The Jungle Book

The Adventures of Bullwhip Griffin

Brighty of the Grand Canyon

The Gnome Mobile

Charlie, the Lonesome Cougar

The Heathens of Kummerow

Jack and the Beanstalk

The Wacky World of Mother Goose

Monkeys, Go Home!

FOREIGN FILMS

*Belle de Jour** FR/IT

Live for Life   FR

2 or 3 Things I Know About Her   FR

Bewitched Love   SPA

Brief Encounters   USSR

Dragon Inn   TAI

Elvira Madigan   SWE

Hamraaz   IND

I Am Curious (Yellow & Blue)   SWE

I Even Met Happy Gypsies   YUG

Japanese Summer: Double Suicide
JPN

Kidnapping, Caucasian Style   USSR

Le Samouraï   JPN

L'immorale   IT

Mouchette   FR

Poor Cow   UK

Samurai Rebellion   JPN

Six Moral Tales series   FR
III. The Collector

The Firemen's Ball   CZE

The Fox   CAN

The Stranger   IT

The Two of Us   FR

The War is Over   FR

The Young Girls of Rochefort   FR

Zatoichi Challenged
Zatoichi the Outlaw
Zatoichi's Cane Sword   JPN

HONORABLE MENTION

A Colt Is My Passport   JPN

Accident   UK

Earth Entranced   BRZ

Hells Angels on Wheels

Massacre Inn   JPN

Samurai Wolf II   JPN

Smashing Time   UK

The Cave of the Silken Web   HK

The Jokers   UK

The Red and the White   HUN

Violated Angels   JPN

Viy   USSR

HORROR & CULT

Branded to Kill   Spiderbaby

David Holzman's Diary   The Love Life of an Octopus

Django, Kill! (If You Live Shoot)   The Vengeance of Fu Manchu

Marketa Lazarova   Uncle Yanco

Playtime   Week End

THIS MOVIE SUCKS

Clambake

<u>NOTES</u>

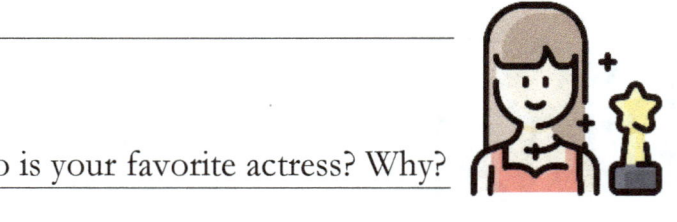

Who is your favorite actress? Why?

1966 AWARD SEASON

A Man for All Seasons*   **[3]**

Blow-Up

The Russians Are Coming,
The Russians Are Coming*

Who's Afraid of Virginia
Woolf?*

A Funny Thing Happened on
the Way to the Forum

Alfie*

Born Free

Gambit

Georgy Girl*

Grand Prix*

Is Paris Burning?

Khartoum

Mister Buddwing

Not With My Wife, You Don't!

Return of the Seven

Seconds

Stop the World - I Want to Get Off

The Fortune Cookie

The Oscar

The Professionals*

The Sand Pebbles*

The Shop on Main Street

The Singing Nun

You're a Big Boy Now

BLOCKBUSTERS

Hawaii

The Blue Max

The Bible:
In the Beginning…

The Good, The Bad and The Ugly

The Group

Fantastic Voyage

The Silencers

Harper

The Wild Angels

Lt. Robin Crusoe, U.S.N.

Torn Curtain

Paradise, Hawaiian Style

Walk Don't Run

CRITICALLY ACCLAIMED

A Man Could Get Killed

Morgan: A Suitable Case for Treatment

Any Wednesday

Ride in the Whirlwind

Case for Treatment

The Appaloosa

Fahrenheit 451

The Shooting

Kill, Baby… Kill

This Property is Condemned

1966

DOCUMENTARIES

The War Game

The Face of a Genius

A Time for Burning

The Forbidden Volcano

Helicopter Canada

The Really Big Family

FOR THE FAMILY & KIDS

Alice in Wonderland*

The Fighting Prince of Donegal

Follow Me, Boys!*

The Great St. Trinian's
Train Robbery

Jimmy, the Boy Wonder

The Magic Serpent

Namu, the Killer Whale

The Man Called Flintstone

The Christmas That Almost Wasn't

The Ugly Dachshund

The Daydreamer

Thunderbirds Are Go

1966

FOREIGN FILMS

A Man and a Woman*   FR

Closely Watched Trains   CZE

The Birds, the Bees and the Italians   IT

War and Peace (66-67)   USSR

Andrei Rublev   USSR

Au Hasard Balthazar   FR

Black Girl   FR/SEN

Black Tight Killers   JPN

Come Drink with Me   HK

Cul-de-sac   UK

Here is Your Life   SWE

Irezumi   JPN

King of Hearts   FR/IT

Law of the Border   TUR

Made in USA   FR

Mademoiselle   FR

Persona   SWE

Pharaoh   POL

Phool Aur Patthar   IND

Signore & Signori   IT

Silence Has No Wings   JPN

The Battles of Algiers   ALG/IT

The Face of Another   JPN

The Monkey Goes West   HK

The Second Souffle   FR

1966

The Sword of Doom   JPN

The Taking of Power by Louis XIV
The Rise of Louis XIV   FR

Tokyo Drifter   JPN

Young Torless   GER

Zatoichi's Pilgrimage
Zatoichi's Vengeance   JPN

HORROR & CULT

A Report on the Party
and the Guests

An Angel for Satan

Daises

Fighting Elegy

Island of Terror

Manos: The Hands of Fate

Rakvickarna

Samurai Wolf

The Brides of Fu Manchu

The Hero

The Pornographers

The Red Angel

<u>NOTES</u>

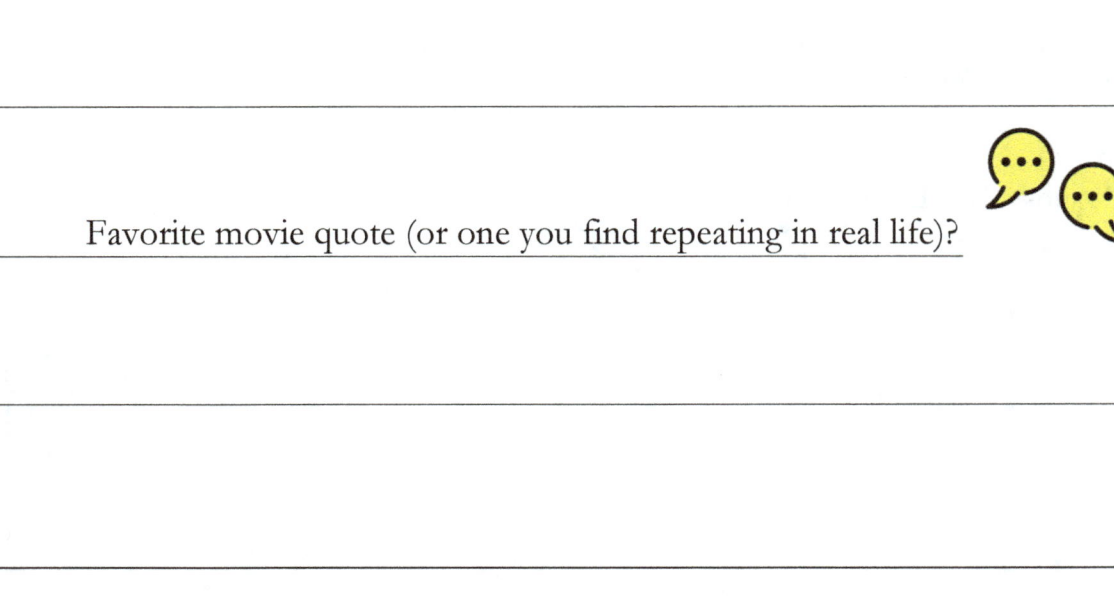

Favorite movie quote (or one you find repeating in real life)?

1965 AWARD SEASON

Doctor Zhivago*

The Knack...
and How to Get It

The Sound of Music*   [2]

A Patch of Blue

A Thousand Clowns

Battle of the Bulge

Boeing (707) Boeing (707)

Casanova 70

Cat Ballou

Harlow

Inside Daisy Clover

King Rat

Morituri

Othello

Ship of Fools

The Agony and the Ecstasy

The Cincinnati Kid

The Collector

The Flight of the Phoenix

The Great Race*

The Sandpiper

The Slender Thread

The Spy Who Came in
From the Cold

The Yellow Rolls-Royce

Those Magnificent Men in
Their Flying Machines*

BLOCKBUSTERS

Shenandoah

Von Ryan's Express

Thunderball

What's New Pussycat?

CRITICALLY ACCLAIMED

A Rage to Live

The Greatest Story Ever Told

Falstaff/Chimes at Midnight

The Hill

Faster, Pussycat! Kill! Kill!

The Loved One

Mudhoney

The Naked Prey

Repulsion

The Nanny

The 10th Victim

Vinyl

DOCUMENTARIES

The Eleanor Roosevelt Story

I'm Going to Ask You to Get Up Out of Your Seat

A King's Story

Let My People Go

Buster Keaton Rides Again

The Battle of the Bulge: The Brave Rifles

Goal! The World Cup

The Forth Road Bridge

FOR THE FAMILY & KIDS

A Charlie Brown Christmas

The Magic World of Topo Gigio

Clarence, the Cross-Eyed Lion

The Man from Button Willow

Funny Things Happen Down Under

Those Calloways

Gulliver's Travels Beyond the Moon

Willy McBean and His Magic Machine

Lemon Grove Kids Meet the Monsters

Zebra in the Kitchen

That Darn Cat!*

FOREIGN FILMS

Darling   UK

Juliet of the Spirits   IT

The Shop of Main Street   CZE

A Fugitive from the Past   JPN

Alphaville   FR/IT

Always Further On   MEX

Golden River   IND

Help!   UK

Illusion of Blood   JPN

Impossible on Saturday   FR

Kwaiden   JPN

Le Bonheur   FR

Loves of a Blonde   CZE

Ninety Degrees in the Shade   UKR

Red Beard   JPN

Story of a Prostitute   JPN

Sword of the Beast   JPN

The Ipcress File   UK

The Leather Boys   UK

The Man Who Had
His Hair Cut Short   BEL

The Mandrake   IT

The Round Up   HUN

Three   YUG

Tokyo Olympiad   JPN

Zatoichi and the Chess Expert
Zatoichi and the Doomed Man
Zatoichi's Revenge   JPN

HORROR & CULT

Pierrot Le Fou   Sins of the Fleshapoids

Shadows of Forgotten Ancestors   The Face of Fu Manchu

Simon of the Desert   The Saragossa Manuscript

THIS MOVIE SUCKS

Monster a Go Go

<u>NOTES</u>

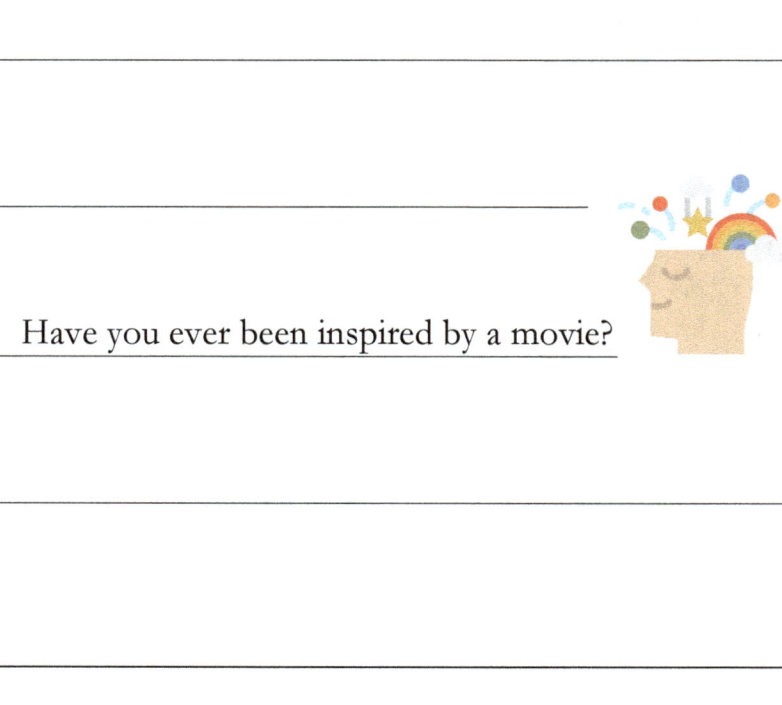

Have you ever been inspired by a movie?

1964 AWARD SEASON

Becket

The Americanization of Emily

*Dr. Strangelove or: How I Learned to Stop Worrying and Love the Bomb**

The Chalk Garden

The Masque of the Red Death

My Fair Lady   **[3]**

The Night of the Iguana

*A Hard Day's Night**

The Pawnbroker

Dear Heart

The Pleasure Seekers

Fail Safe

The Train

Father Goose*

The Unsinkable Molly Brown*

Hush… Hush, Sweet Charlotte

The World of Henry Orient

Marnie

Topkaki

Rio Conchos

Zorba the Greek

Seven Days in May

Zulu

BLOCKBUSTERS

Goldfinger **

The Best Man

A Shot in the Dark

The Carpetbaggers

One Potato, Two Potato

What a Way to Go!

That Man from Rio

CRITICALLY ACCLAIMED

7 Faces of Dr. Lao

Robin and the 7 Hoods

A House is Not a Home

Robinson Crusoe on Mars

Cheyenne Autumn

The Killers

Circus World

The Lively Set

Fate is the Hunter

The Naked Kiss

Kisses for My President

The Pumpkin Eater

Nothing But a Man

Where Love Has Gone

DOCUMENTARIES

World Without Sun

The Finest Hours

Four Days in November

FOR THE FAMILY & KIDS

Mary Poppins*

Island of the Blue Dolphins

A Tiger Walks

The Misadventures of Merlin Jones

Emil and the Detectives

The Moon-Spinners

Flipper's New Adventure

The Three Lives of Thomasina

Hey There, It's Yogi Bear!

FOREIGN FILMS

Marriage Italian Style   IT

Band of Outsiders   FR

The Umbrellas of Cherbourg
GER/FR

Before The Revolution   IT

Black God, White Devil   BRZ

Adventures of Zatoichi JPN

Charulata   IND

1964

Circle of Love   FR

Dear John   SWE

Diamonds of the Night   CZE

Diary of a Chambermaid   FR/IT

Dry Summer   TUR

Fight, Zatoichi, Fight   JPN

Gate of Flesh   JPN

Gertrud   DAN

Hamlet   USSR

I Am Cuba   USSR/CUB

Intentions of Murder/
Unholy Desire   JPN

Pale Flower   JPN

Sallah Shabati   ISR

Seduced and Abandoned   IT

The Demon/Onibaba   JPN

The Gospel According
to Saint Matthew   IT/FR

The Leather Boys   UK

The Red Desert   IT

The Soft Skin   FR

Three Outlaw Samurai   JPN

Woman in the Dunes   JPN

Zatoichi & the Chest of Gold
Zatoichi's Flashing Sword   JPN

HORROR & CULT

At Midnight, I'll Take Your Soul

Lemonade Joe

Blood and Black Lace

Scorpio Rising

Dog Star Man: Parts III & IV

Strait-Jacket

THIS MOVIE SUCKS

Santa Claus Conquers the Martians

The Horror of Party Beach

The Creeping Terror

The Incredible Strange Creatures
Who Stopped Living and Became
Mixed Up Zombies

1964

<u>NOTES</u>

Share a movie that always brings you to tears and the reason behind it.

1963 AWARD SEASON

The Cardinal*

Tom Jones*   [3]

55 Days at Peking*

A New Kind of Love

A Ticklish Affair

America America

Bye Bye Birdie*

Captain Newman, M.D.

Come Blow Your Horn*

Hud

Irma la Douce*

It's a Mad, Mad, Mad, Mad World*

Lilies of the Field

Love with the Proper Stranger

Papa's Delicate Condition

The Balcony

The Birds*

The Caretakers

The Conjugal Bed

The Great Escape*

The Haunting

The Paper Man

The Prize

This Sporting Life

Twilight of Honor

Under the Yum Tree

BLOCKBUSTERS

Cleopatra **

Move Over, Darling

From Russia with Love

My Life to Live

Summer Magic

Charade

The Pink Panther

Donovan's Reef

The Thrill of It All

Fun in Acapulco

McLintock!

CRITICALLY ACCLAIMED

Billy Liar

The Mouse on the Moon

Blonde Cobra

The Silence

Lord of the Flies

The V.I.Ps

Shock Corridor

The Wheeler Dealers

The Cool World

Toys in the Attic

DOCUMENTARIES

Robert Frost: A Lover's Quarrel with the World

The Human Dutch

The Link and the Chain

Over There, 1914-18

The Yanks are Coming

To Die in Madrid

FOR THE FAMILY & KIDS

Captain Sinbad

Spencer's Mountain

Flipper

The Courtship of Eddie's Father

Jason and the Argonauts

The Incredible Journey

Lassie's Great Adventure

The Sword in the Stone*

Miracle of the White Stallions

The Three Lives of Thomasina

Savage Sam

When the Cat Comes

Son of Flubber

FOREIGN FILMS

8 1/2   IT/FR

Any Number Can Win   FR

The Leopard   IT/FR

Yesterday, Today and
Tomorrow   IT

An Actor's Revenge   JPN

Baji   PAK

Barren Lives   BRZ

Bay of Angels   FR

Contempt   FR/IT

Heads Over the City   IT

High and Low   JPN

Judex   FR

Los Tarantos   SPA

Mediterranean   FR

Muriel, or The Time of Return   FR

New Tale of Zatoichi   JPN

Passenger   POL

Raven's End   SWE

Suzanne's Career   FR

The Bakery Girl of Monceau   FR

The Big City/Mahanagar   IND

The Executioner   SPA

The Fiancés   IT

The Fire Within   FR

The House in Black   IRN

The Immortal One   FR

The Insect Woman   JPN

The Little Soldier   FR

The Organizer   IT/FR/YUG

The Red Lanterns   GRC

The Servant   UK

This Sporting Life   UK

To Bed or Not to Bed   IT

Twin Sisters of Kyoto   JPN

Winter Light   SWE

Youth of the Beast   JPN

Zatoichi on the Road
Zatoichi: The Fugitive   JPN

HORROR & CULT

13 Frightened Girls!

Blood Feast

Dog Star Man: Part II

Flaming Creatures

X: The Man with the X-Ray Eyes

<u>NOTES</u>

Favorite romantic movie? Favorite couple?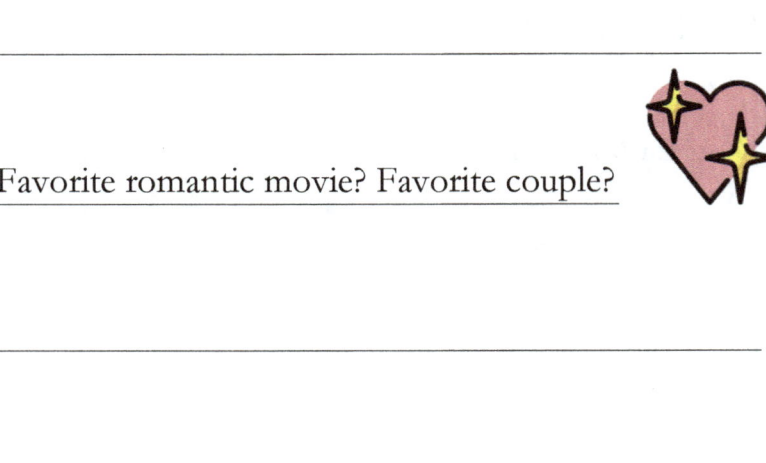

1962 AWARD SEASON

Lawrence of Arabia* **[3]**

That Touch of Mink*

The Music Man*

Billy Rose's Jumbo

Boys' Night Out

David and Lisa

Days of Wine and Roses

Freud: The Secret Passion

Girls! Girls! Girls!

Hemingway's Adventures of a Young Man

If a Man Answers

Jumbo

Lolita*

Long Day's Journey Into Night

Mutiny on the Bounty*

Period of Adjustment

The Best of Enemies

The Chapman Report

The Inspector

The Loneliness of the Long Distance Runner

The Manchurian Candidate

The Miracle Worker

The Wonderful World of the Brothers Grimm*

To Kill a Mockingbird*

BLOCKBUSTERS

How the West Was Won

Kid Galahad

The Longest Day **

State Fair

The Interns

Dr. No

The Man Who Shot Liberty Vallance

Gypsy

The Premature Burial

Hatari!

In Search of the Castaways

CRITICALLY ACCLAIMED

Birdman of Alcatraz

Salvatore Giuliano

Gigot

The Exterminating Angel

My Son, The Hero

The Pigeon That Took Rome

Phaedra

The Trial

Pressure Point

Walk on the Wild Side

FOR THE FAMILY & KIDS

Big Red

Bon Voyage!

Gay Purr-ee

Heaven and Earth Magic

Jack the Giant Killer

Little Red Riding Hood and
Tom Thumb vs. the Monsters

The Magic Sword

The Two Who Stole the Moon

FOREIGN FILMS

Keeper of Promises   BRZ

Sundays & Cybele   FR/AUT

A Dog's Life   IT

A Kind of Loving   UK

An Autumn Afternoon   JPN

Animas Trujano:
The Important Man   MEX

Billy Budd   UK

Cleo from 5 to 7   FR

Electra   GRC

Harakiri   JPN

Ivan's Childhood   USSR

Jules and Jim   FR

Knife in the Water   POL

La Jetée   FR

Le Doulos   FR

Mafioso   IT

Mamma Rosa   IT

Mondo Cane   IT

My Life to Live   FR

Pitfall   JPN

Sanjuro   JPN

The East Life   IT

The Eclipse   IT

The Fabulous Baron Munchausen   CZE

The Four Days of Naples   IT

The Grim Reaper   IT

The L Shaped Room   UK

The Tale of Zatoichi   JPN

Tiyucan   MEX

HORROR & CULT

Carnival of Souls

Dogstar Man Part I

Experiment in Terror

What Ever Happened to Baby Jane?

Zotz!

THIS MOVIE SUCKS

Eegah

<u>NOTES</u>

What is your favorite movie date night experience?

1961 AWARD SEASON

A Majority of One*

The Guns of Navarone*

The Hustler

West Side Story   [2]

A Raisin in the Sun

Babes in Toyland

Breakfast at Tiffany's*

Bridge to the Sun

Claudelle Inglish

Fanny*

Flower Drum Song*

Judgment at Nuremberg

One Eyed Jacks

One, Two, Three

Pocketful of Miracles*

Splendor in the Grass

Summer and Smoke

The Children's Hour

The Exiles

The Ladies Man

The Mark

The Misfits

The Pleasure of His Company

The Roman Spring of Mrs. Stone

Town Without Pity

BLOCKBUSTERS

One Hundred and
One Dalmatians **

La Dolce Vita

Lover Come Back

Blue Hawaii

Return to Peyton Place

Come September

The Absent-Minded Professor

El Cid

The Parent Trap

King of Kings

CRITICALLY ACCLAIMED

Bachelor in Paradise

Samson

Blast of Silence

Something Wild

Devil at 4 O'Clock

The Deadly Companions

Girl with a Suitcase

The Hoodlum Priest

Pit and the Pendulum

Time of the Heathen

Placido

Two Rode Together

Underworld USA

Whistle Down the Wind

FOR THE FAMILY & KIDS

Boy Who Caught a Crook

Snow White and the Three Stooges

Greyfriars Bobby

The Legend of Lobo

Misty

Tomboy and the Champ

Nikki, Wild Dog of the North

FOREIGN FILMS

Divorce Italian Style   IT

Dancing in the Rain   SVK

The Long Absence   FR

Fists in the Pocket   IT

Through a Glass Darkly   SWE

Gunga Jumna   IT

Viridiana   SPA/MEX

Harry and the Butler   DNK

Il Posto   IT

A Taste of Honey   UK

Immortal Love   JPN

A Woman is a Woman   FR

La Notte   IT/FR

Last Year at Marienbad   FR/IT

Leon Morin, Priest   FR

Lola   FR/IT

Obaltan   KOR

Paris Belongs to Us   FR

Striped Trip   USSR

The Best of Enemies   IT

The Good Soldier Schweik   GER

*The Human Condition 3:
A Soldier's Prayer*   JPN

Victim   UK

Yojimbo   JPN

HORROR & CULT

Accattone

Ada

Carry on Regardless

Goodbye Again

Master of the World

Mothra

Mr. Topaze

Murder, She Said

Mysterious Island

No Love for Johnnie

Prelude (Dog Star Man)

Taste of Fear

The Colossus of Rhodes

The Curse of the Werewolf

The Innocents   X-15

Too Late Blues

THIS MOVIE SUCKS

Doctor' Blood's Coffin   Reptilicus

Gorgo   The Beast of Yucca Flats

<u>NOTES</u>

What's the most visually stunning film you've ever seen?

1960 AWARD SEASON

Song Without End

Spartacus*

The Apartment* [3]

Bells Are Ringing

BUtterfield 8*

Can-Can

Cimarron

Conspiracy of Hearts

Elmer Gantry

Exodus*

Hand in Hand

Inherit the Wind

It Started in Naples

Let's Make Love

Midnight Lace*

Murder, Inc.*

Never on Sunday

Our Man in Havana

Pepe

Sons and Lovers

Sunrise at Campobello

The Alamo*

The Angry Silence

The Dark at the Top of the Stairs*

The Entertainer

1960

The Facts of Life

The Time Machine

The Grass Is Greener

The World of Suzie Wong*

The Rise and Fall of Legs Diamond

Who Was That Lady?

The Sundowners

BLOCKBUSTERS

Psycho **

North to Alaska

13 Ghosts

Ocean's 11

Cinderfella

Please Don't Eat the Daisies

Comanche Station

The Little Shop of Horrors

From the Terrace

The Magnificent Seven

Jazz Boat

Wild River

DOCUMENTARIES

Rebel in Paradise

The Horse with the Flying Tail

FOR THE FAMILY & KIDS

Swiss Family Robinson

The Adventures of Huckleberry Finn

Alakazam the Great

The Boy and the Pirates

David and Goliath

The Hound That Thought
He Was a Raccoon

Kidnapped

Those Calloways

Pollyanna*

Toby Tyler

Ten Who Dared

FOREIGN FILMS

La Dolce Vita   IT/FR

The Truth   FR

The Virgin Spring   SWE

Two Women   IT/FR

Black Sunday   IT

Breathless   FR

Eyes Without a Face   FR/IT

Far from the Mother Land*   USSR

Les Bonnes Femmes   FR/IT

Macario   MEX

Peeping Tom   UK

Purple Noon   FR

Rocco and His Brothers   IT/FR

Saturday Night
and Sunday Morning   UK

Shoot the Piano Player   FR

The Bad Sleep Well   JPN

The Cloud-Capped Star   IND

The Great Mughal*   IND

The Hole   FR

The Housemaid   KOR

The Naked Island   JPN

The Ninth Circle   YUG

*The Orphic Trilogy 3:
Testament of Orpheus*   FR

The Trails of Oscar Wilde   UK

Zazie in the Metro   FR

When a Woman Ascends the Stairs
JPN

HONORABLE MENTION

Flaming Star

The Sign of Zorro

Guns of the Timberland

Tunes of Glory

Sergeant Rutledge

Visit to a Small Planet

The Fugitive Kind

HORROR & CULT

Heller in Pink Tights

House of Usher

Horrors of Spider Island

Village of the Damned

<u>NOTES</u>

If you could step into the world of any movie, which one would it be and why?

1959 AWARD SEASON

Ben-Hur   [3]

Porgy and Bess

Some Like It Hot*

A Private's Affair

Anatomy of a Murder*

But Not for Me

Career

Li'l Abner

Middle of the Night

North by Northwest*

Odds Against Tomorrow

On the Beach*

Operation Petticoat*

Pillow Talk*

Say One for Me

Suddenly, Last Summer*

Take a Giant Step

The Diary of Anne Frank

The Five Pennies

The Nun's Story*

The Young Philadelphians*

BLOCKBUSTERS

Imitation of Life

Sleeping Beauty

Journey to the Center of the Earth

The Hound of the Baskervilles

Look Back in Anger

The Mouse That Roared

No Name on the Bullet

The Shaggy Dog

Rio Bravo

DOCUMENTARIES

Serengeti Shall Not Die

The Race for Space

CRITICALLY ACCLAIMED

Compulsion

Shadows

Ride Lonesome

The Best of Everything

FOR THE FAMILY & KIDS

1001 Arabian Nights

Darby O'Gill and the Little People

A Dog of Flanders

Magic Boy

FOREIGN FILMS

Ballad of a Soldier USSR

Les Cousins FR

Black Orpheus   FR

Letter Never Sent USSR

Odd Obsession JPN

Paw DNK

Room at the Top   UK

Pickpocket FR

The Bridge GER

The 400 Blows FR

Fires of the Plain JPN

The Apu Trilogy: World of Apu IND

General Della Rovere IT

The Great War IT

Hiroshima Mon Amour FR/JPN

The Human Condition
I. No Greater Love
II. Road to Eternity   JPN

Khovanshcina USSR

Violent Summer   IT

HORROR & CULT

Corridors of Blood

Santa Claus

First Man in Space

The Atomic Submarine

House on Haunted Hill

The Tingler

<u>NOTES</u>

What movie should everyone watch at least once in their lifetime?

1958 AWARD SEASON

A Night to Remember

Auntie Mame*

Gigi*

The Defiant Ones

A Time to Love and A Time to Die

Bell, Book and Candle

Cat on a Hot Tin Roof*

Damn Yankees

Home Before Dark

Houseboat

I Want to Live!

Indiscreet*

Lonelyhearts

Me and the Colonel

Separate Tables

Teacher's Pet

The Big Country

The Inn of the Sixth Happiness*

The Perfect Furlough

The Proud Rebel

The Tunnel of Love

Tom Thumb

1958

BLOCKBUSTERS

South Pacific **

The 7th Voyage of Sinbad

Anna Lucasta

The Blob

No Time for Sergeants

The Vikings

Rally 'Round the Flag, Boys

The Young Lions

Some Came Running

Touch of Evil

CRITICALLY ACCLAIMED

Chase a Crooked Shadow

The Left Handed Gun

Cry Terror!

The Lineup

King Creole

The Long, Hot Summer

Murder by Contract

The Matchmaker

Party Girl

The Old Man and The Sea

The Fly

Violent Playground

1958

DOCUMENTARIES

White Wilderness

Antarctic Crossing

Psychiatric Nursing

The Hidden World

FOREIGN FILMS

Aren't We Wonderful?   GER

Girl and the River   FR

My Uncle   FR

Rosemarie   GER

The Road a Year Long YUG

Arms and the Man   GER

Ashes and Diamonds   POL

Big Deal on Madonna Street   IT

Cairo Station   EGY

Elevator to the Gallows FR

Fiend Without a Face UK

Giants and Toys   JPN

Invention for Destruction   CZE

La Venganza   SPA

Le Beau Serge   FR

The Ballad of Narayama JPN

The Hidden Fortress JPN

The Loves   FR

The Magician   SWE

The Music Room   IND

The Village of the River   NLD

The Usual Unidentified Thieves   IT

Vengeance   SPA

<u>NOTES</u>

Favorite comedy?

1957 AWARD SEASON

Cole Porter's Les Girls

The Bridge on the River Kwai [3]

12 Angry Men

A Hatful of Rain

Desk Set

Don't Go Near the Water*

Gunfight at the O.K. Corral*

Heaven Knows, Mr. Allison

Love in the Afternoon

My Man Godfrey

Pal Joey*

Paths of Glory

Peyton Place*

Raintree County*

Sayonara*

Silk Stockings

Sweet Smell of Success

The Seventh Seal

The Spirit of St. Louis*

The Story of Esther Costello

This Could Be the Night

Will Success Spoil Rock Hunter?

Witness for the Prosecution`

<u>BLOCKBUSTERS</u>

A Farewell to Arms

An Affair to Remember

Curse of Frankenstein

Curse of the Demon

Fear Strikes Out

Island in the Sun

Man of a Thousand Faces

Old Yeller

Run of the Arrow

Search for Paradise

The Enemy Below

The Invisible Shrinking Man

The Monolith Monsters

The One That Got Away

The Three Faces of Eve

The Tin Star

<u>CRITICALLY ACCLAIMED</u>

3:10 to Yuma

A Face in the Crowd

Battle Hymn

Forty Guns

DOCUMENTARIES

Albert Schweitzer

Martha Graham: Dance on Film

FOR THE FAMILY & KIDS

Johnny Tremaine

The Snow Queen

The Singing Ringing Tree

FOREIGN FILMS

Nights of Cabiria　IT

A Sun-Tribe Myth from the Bakumatsu Era　JPN

The Confessions of Felix Krull　GER

Gates of Paris　FR

The Cranes are Flying USSR

Kanal　POL

Mayabazar　IND

Tizoc　MEX

Mother India　IND

Wild Strawberries　SWE

Nine Lives　NOR

Woman in a Dressing Gown　UK

The Devil Strikes at Night　GER

White Nights　FR

Yellow Crow　JPN

NOTES

What's the last movie that made you laugh uncontrollably?

1956 AWARD SEASON

Around the World in 80 Days **[2]**

Friendly Persuasion

The King and I*

Anastasia

Baby Doll

Bundle of Joy

Bus Stop

Forbidden Planet

Giant*

Lust for Life

The Bad Seed

The Bold and the Brave

The Court Jester

The Opposite Sex

The Rainmaker

The Searchers

The Solid Gold Cadillac

The Teahouse of the August Moon*

War and Peace*

Written on the Wind

BLOCKBUSTERS

The Ten Commandments **

Seven Wonders of the World

Carousel

The Eddy Duchin Story

High Society

Trapeze

CRITICALLY ACCLAIMED

1984

Love Me Tender

23 Paces to Baker Street

Somebody Up There Likes Me

Attack

Tea and Sympathy

Battle Hymn

The Girl Can't Help It

Bigger Than Life

The Killing

Blazing the Overland Trail

The Man Who Knew Too Much

Dance with Me, Henry

The Revolt of Mamie Stover

Invasion of the Body Snatchers

The Wrong Man

Jubal

Three Violent People

DOCUMENTARIES

The Silent World

The Naked Eye

On the Bowery

Torero!

FOR THE FAMILY & KIDS

Davy Crockett and the River Pirates

The Red Balloon

The Brave One

ANIMATED SHORT

Magoo's Puddle Jumper

The Jaywalker

Gerald McBoing-Boing on
Planet Moo

FOREIGN FILMS

Gervaise   FR

Crazed Fruit   JPN

A Man Escaped   FR

Godzilla: King of the Monsters JPN

And God Created Woman   FR

Harp of Burma   JPN

1956

O Drakos   GRC

Qivitoq   DNK

Samurai III:
Duel at Ganryu Island JPN

The Apu Trilogy: Aparajito   IND

The Burmese Harp   JPN

The Captain of Kopenick   GER

The Third Key   UK

LIVE ACTION SHORT

Crashing the Water Barrier

The Bespoke Overcoat

Cow Dog

I Never Forget a Face

Samoa

The Dark Wave

Time Stood Still

THIS MOVIE SUCKS

Fire Maidens from Outer Space

The Conqueror

<u>NOTES</u>

Favorite foreign film? Do you enjoy films from a particular country?

1955 AWARD SEASON

East of Eden

Guys and Dolls*

Marty **[2]**

Bad Day at Black Rock

Blackboard Jungle*

Dangerous Curves

Interrupted Melody

It's Always Fair Weather

Love Is a Many-Splendored Thing*

Picnic*

Queen Bee

Rebel Without a Cause*

Stella

Summertime

The Big Combo

The Man with the Golden Arm

The Rose Tattoo

The Seven Little Foys

The Seven Year Itch*

The Trouble with Harry

Trial

We're No Angels

BLOCKBUSTERS

Cinerama Holiday

Mister Roberts **

Artists and Models

Battle Cry

I'll Cry Tomorrow

King of the Carnival

Kiss Me Deadly

Oklahoma!

Strategic Air Command

The Ladykillers

The Sea Chase

To Catch a Thief

To Hell and Back

CRITICALLY ACCLAIMED

All That Heaven Allows

Bloody Alley

Bob the Gambler

Confidential Report

Crashout

Hit the Deck

My Sister Eileen

The Complete Mr. Arkadin

The Desperate Hours

The Eternal Breasts

The View from Pompey's Head   Wichita

FOR THE FAMILY & KIDS

Lady and the Tramp*   John and Julie

A Man Called Peter   The Court Jester*

Davy Crockett,   The Littlest Outlaw
King of the Wild Frontier

The Stolen Airliner

ANIMATED SHORT

Speedy Gonzales   No Hunting

Good Will to Men   The Legend of Rockabye Point

FOREIGN FILMS

Eyes of Children   JPN

Richard III   UK   **[2]**

Sons, Mothers and a
General GER

Stella   GRC

The Word   DNK

A Generation   POL

Death of a Cyclist   SPA

Diabolique   FR

French Cancan   FR/IT

Journey to the Beginning of Time   CZE

La Pointe Courte   FR

Lola Montes   FR/GER

Night and Fog   FR

Rififi   FIN

Shree 420   IND

Smiles of a Summer Night   SWE

The Apu Trilogy: Pather Panchali   IND

The Devil's General   GER

The Girlfriends   IT

The Plot to Assassinate Hitler   GER

The Unknown Soldier   FIN

Wajda: Three War Films (1955-58)
POL

<u>NOTES</u>

Do you prefer subtitles or dubbed audio?

1954 AWARD SEASON

Carmen Jones

On the Waterfront   [2]

A Star is Born*

An Inspector Calls

Brigadoon

Broken Lance

Executive Suite

Genevieve

Knock on Wood

Magnificent Obsession*

Robinson Crusoe

Sabrina

Seven Brides for Seven Brothers*

The Barefoot Contessa

The Caine Mutiny*

The Country Girl*

The High and the Mighty*

The Naked Jungle

The Sheep Has Five Legs

There's No Business Like
Show Business*

Three Coins in the Fountain*

BLOCKBUSTERS

20,000 Leagues
Under the Sea

Rear Window **

White Christmas

Dial M For Murder

Hobson's Choice

Johnny Guitar

Riot in Cell Block 11

Salt of the Earth

The Glenn Miller Story

The Long, Long Trailer

Them!

CRITICALLY ACCLAIMED

A Time Out of War(s)

Creature From the Black Lagoon

Four Guns to the Border

Phffft!

The Inauguration of
the Pleasure Dome

DOCUMENTARIES

Helen Keller in Her Story

The Stratford Adventure

The Vanishing Prairie

FOR THE FAMILY & KIDS

Animal Farm

Hansel and Gretel
(dir. by Walter Janssen)

Arie Prerie

Mother Holly

Hansel and Gretel
(dir. by Fritz Genschow)

Return to Treasure Island

ANIMATED SHORT

When Magoo Flew

Sandy Claws

Crazy Mixed Up Pup

Touché, Pussy Cat!

Pigs Is Pigs

FOREIGN FILMS

La Strada IT

Godzilla JPN

Samurai: The Legend of Musaski JPN

Nagin IND

The Lady of the Camalias ARG

Royal Affairs in Versailles FR

Sansho the Bailiff JPN

Twenty-Four Eyes JPN

Senso / The Wanton Countess IT

A Story from…
Chikamatsu Monogatari JPN

Seven Samurai JPN

Bread, Love and Dreams IT

The Divided Heart UK

Ulysses IT

Doctor in the House JPN

Voyage to Italy IT

Don't Touch the Loot FR/IT

What is Your Name? Part 3 JPN

<u>NOTES</u>

Favorite musical? Favorite song from a movie?

1953 AWARD SEASON

<mark>From Here to Eternity</mark>

All the Brothers Were Valiant

Call Me Madam

Crazylegs

Dream Wife

Forever Female

Hell and High Water

Hondo

It Came from Outer Space

Julius Caesar

Kiss Me Kate

Knights of the Round Table

Lili

Little Boy Lost

Martin Luther

Mogambo

Money from Home

*Pickup on South Street**

Roman Holiday

Shane

Small Town Girl

So Big

Stalag 17*

The Actress

The Big Heat

The Caddy

The Captain's Paradise	The Man from the Alamo
The Cruel Sea	The Mississippi Gambler
The Desert Rats	The Moon is Blue
The Earrings of Madame De...	The Naked Spur*
The Egyptian	Titanic*
The Glory Brigade	Torch Song
The Kid from Left Field	

BLOCKBUSTERS

The Robe	Indiscretion of an American Wife
Angel Face	Niagara
Gentlemen Prefer Blondes	Salome
House of Wax	The Band Wagon
How to Marry a Millionaire	The Golden Coach
I Confess	The War of The Worlds

The Wild One

CRITICALLY ACCLAIMED

Arrowhead

Robot Monster

Beneath the 12-Mile Reef

Take the High Ground!

Calamity Jane

The Heart of the Matter

Crime Wave

The Kidnappers

Folly to be Wise

The Man Between

Houdini

The President's Lady

Miss Sadie Thompson

DOCUMENTARIES

A Queen is Crowned

The Golden Age of Television
Various

The Sea Around Us

The Living Desert

By Brakhage: An Anthology

Young Bess

The Conquest of Everest

FOR THE FAMILY & KIDS

Peter Pan

The 5000 Fingers of Dr. T

Confidentially Connie

The Sword and the Rose

Rob Roy: The Highland Rogue

White Mane

ANIMATED SHORT

Toot, Whistle, Plunk
and Boom

From A to Z-Z-Z-Z

Rugged Bear

Christopher Crumpet

The Tell-Tale Heart

FOREIGN FILMS

Gate of Hell   JPN

Genevieve   UK

No Way Back   GER

The Wages of Fear   IT/FR   **[2]**

Beat the Devil   UK/IT

I Vitelloni   IT

Madame De...   IT/FR

Monsieur Hulot's Holiday   FR

Sawdust and Tinsel*   SWE

Stage and Spectacle:
Three Films by Jean Renoir   FR

Summer with Monika   SWE

Tokyo Story   JPN

Ugetsu Monogatari   JPN

<u>NOTES</u>

Favorite film musician? Favorite composer?

1952 AWARD SEASON

The Greatest Show on Earth   [2]

With a Song in My Heart

5 Fingers

Anything Can Happen

Assignment: Paris

Come Back, Little Sheba*

Don't Bother to Knock

Hans Christian Andersen*

High Noon

I'll See You in My Dreams

Ivanhoe*

Monkey Business

Moulin Rouge*

My Cousin Rachel

My Six Convicts

Pat and Mike

Singin' in the Rain

Stars and Stripes Forever

The Bad and the Beautiful

The Four Poster

The Happy Time

The Quiet Man

The Thief

Viva Zapata!

BLOCKBUSTERS

This is Cinerama

The Big Sky

Breaking the Sound Barrier

The Marrying Kind

Jumping Jacks

The Snows of Kilimanjaro

Sailor Beware

The Stooge

Sudden Fear

CRITICALLY ACCLAIMED

Above and Beyond

I Believe in You

Affair in Trinidad

It Grows on Trees

Bwana Devil

Just for You

Carrie

Limelight

Deadline USA

My Pal Gus

Flat Top

My Son John

Has Anybody Seen My Gal

Othello

Park Row	The Card
Room for One More	The Merry Widow
Ruby Gentry	The Pickwick Papers
Scandal Sheet	The Sniper
Son of Paleface	

DOCUMENTARIES

The Hoaxters

Navajo

ANIMATED SHORT

Johann Mouse

Pink and Blue Blues

Little Johnny Jet

Romance of Transportation

Madeline

FOREIGN FILMS

Forbidden Games   FR   **[2]**

The Sound Barrier   UK   **[2]**

Two Cents Worth of Hope   IT

Aan   IND

Angels One Five   UK

Europa '51   IT

Fanfan la Tulipe   FR/IT

Golden Helmet   FR

Himeyurino To   JPN

House of Pleasure   FR

Ikiru   JPN

Little World of Don Camillo   FR/IT

Mandy   UK

The Boy Kumasenu   GHA

The Flavor of Green Tea Over Rice   JPN

The Golden Coach   FR/IT

The Importance of Being Earnest   UK

The Life of Oharu   JPN

The Romance of Transportation in Canada   CAN

The White Sheik   IT

Umberto D   IT

<u>NOTES</u>

Which soundtrack is permanently etched in your mind?

1951 AWARD SEASON

A Place in the Sun*

An American in Paris* [2]

A Streetcar Named Desire*

Ace in the Hole

Alice in Wonderland

Angels in the Outfield

Bright Victory

David and Bathsheba*

Death of a Salesman

Decision Before Dawn

Detective Story

Fourteen Hours

Go for Broke!

Golden Girl

Here Comes the Groom

I Want You

I'll See You in My Dreams

Kind Lady

No Resting Place

On the Riviera

Rich, Young and Pretty

Royal Wedding

Show Boat*

Strangers on a Train

The African Queen*

The Blue Veil

1951

The Browning Version

The Day the Earth Stood Still

The Great Caruso*

The House on Telegraph Hill

The Lavender Hill Mob

The Magic Box

The Magic Garden

The Man in the White Suit

The Mating Season

The Model and the Marriage Broker

The Small Miracle

The Strip

The Tales of Hoffmann

The Tall Target

The Thing (From Another World)

The Well

Too Young to Kiss

Two Tickets to Broadway

When Worlds Collide

1951

BLOCKBUSTERS

Quo Vadis **

Four in a Jeep

Distant Drums

That's My Boy

Father's Little Dividend

CRITICALLY ACCLAIMED

The Tragedy of Othello:
The Moor of Venice

On Dangerous Ground

Pandora and the Flying Dutchman

A Christmas Carol

The Enforcer

Bedtime for Bonzo

The Red Badge of Courage

Early Summer

The River

Miss Julie

Westward the Women

Never Take No for an Answer
(The Small Miracle)

DOCUMENTARIES

Kon-Tiki

Out of True

I Was a Communist for the FBI

Royal Journey

Oil for the Twentieth Century

Tomorrow is Another Day

FOREIGN FILMS

Miracle in Milan   IT

La Poison   FR

Miss Julie   SWE

Outcast of the Islands   UK

Anna   IT

Pool of London   UK

Awaara   IND

Rapast   JPN

Cry, the Beloved Country   UK

Scoorge   UK

Diary of a Country Priest   FR

The Red Inn   FR

Edward and Caroline   FR

The Tale of Genji*   JPN

In Peaceful Time   USSR

White Corridors   UK

ANIMATED SHORT

The Two Mouseketeers

Rooty Toot Toot

Lambert the Sheepish Lion

HORROR & CULT

The Prowler

Victims of Sin

The Strange Madame

<u>NOTES</u>

Quick!! Write down as many 'movie words' as you know!

1950 AWARD SEASON

All About Eve   [2]

Sunset Boulevard

A Life of Her Own

Annie Get Your Gun*

Born Yesterday*

Broken Arrow*

Caged

Captain Carey, USA

Cyrano de Bergerac

Destination Moon

Father of the Bride*

Harvey

I'll Get By

King Solomon's Mines*

Louisa

Mister 880

Mystery Street

No Sad Songs for Me

No Way Out

Our Very Own

September Affair

Singing Guns

The Asphalt Jungle

The Flame and the Arrow

The Gunfighter

The Magnificent Yankee

The Men

The Toast of New Orleans

The West Point Story

Three Little Words

Trio

Wabash Avenue

When Willie Comes
Marching Home

BLOCKBUSTERS

Samson and Delilah **

At War with the Army

Cheaper by the Dozen

Cinderella

Gone to Earth

Madeleine

Night and the City

Rio Grande

So Long at the Fair

Stage Fright

The Damned Don't Cry

Treasure Island

Where the Sidewalk Ends

CRITICALLY ACCLAIMED

Gun Crazy

The Furies

In a Lonely Place

The Lawless/The Dividing Line

Panic in the Streets

The Mudlark

Stromboli

The Sound of Fury

The Breaking Point

Variety Lights

The File on Thelma Jordan

Winchester '73

DOCUMENTARIES

The Titan:
Story of Michelangelo

The Mountain is Green

The Vatican

Inland Waterways

With These Hands

Life Begins Tomorrow

FOREIGN FILMS

La Ronde   FR

Rashomon   JPN

The Blue Lamp   UK   **[2]**

Chance of a Lifetime   UK

God Needs Man   FR

In Peaceful Time   USSR

Beauty and the Devil   IT

The Terrible Children   FR

Morning Departure   UK

Seven Days to Noon   UK

State Secret   UK

Sunday in August   IT

The Flowers of St. Francis   IT

The Orphic Trilogy 2: Orpheus   FR

The Forgotten Ones   MEX

The Wooden Horse   UK

The Young and The Damned   MEX

ANIMATED SHORT

Gerald McBoing-Boing

Trouble Indemnity

Jerry's Cousin

<u>NOTES</u>

What movie star would you like to hang out with in real life?

1949 AWARD SEASON

All the King's Men   [2]

The Third Man

A Letter to Three Wives

Adam's Rib

Battleground*

Beyond the Forest

Champion

Come to the Stable

Death of a Salesman

Edward My Son

Gun Crazy

Hour of Glory / The Small Back Room

Intruder in the Dust

Kind Hearts and Coronets

Little Women*

Look for the Silver Lining

Mighty Joe Young

Mother Is a Freshman

On the Town

Pinky*

Prince of Foxes

Rope of Sand

Sand

Sands of Iwo Jima*

So Dear to My Heart

Tension

1949

The Barkleys of Broadway

The Window*

The Hasty Heart

Thieves' Highway

The Heiress

Tulsa

The Inspector General

Twelve O'Clock High

The Reckless Moment

White Heat

The Red Danube

BLOCKBUSTERS

Jolson Sings Again

Mr. Belvedere Goes to College

Anna Lucasta

Neptune's Daughter

D.O.A. Tale About a Soldier

Sorrowful Jones

I Was a Male War Bride

The Stratton Story

DOCUMENTARIES

Daybreak in Udi

Sardinia Project

Crossroads of Life

The Cornish Engine

Drug Addict

The Liver Fluke in Great Britain

Island of the Lagoon

The People Between

Kenji Comes Home

Visit to Picasso

Report on the Refugee Problem

FOREIGN FILMS

The Walls of Malapaga   FR/IT

Passport to Pimlico   UK

A Run for Your Money   UK

Stray Dog   JPN

Bitter Rice   IT

Such a Pretty Little Beach   FR

Flame of My Love   JPN

The Big Day   FR

Late Spring   JPN

The Passionate Friends   UK

Once a Jolly Swagman   UK

The Queen of Spades   UK

1949

The Silence of the Sea   FR

Whiskey Galore!   UK

Under Capricorn   UK

ANIMATED SHORT

For Scent-imental Reasons

Magic Fluke

Canary Row

Toy Tinkers

Hatch Up Your Troubles

The Adventures of Ichabod
and Mr. Toad

<u>NOTES</u>

If you could invite any movie character to dinner, who would it be & why?

1948 AWARD SEASON

Hamlet   [3]

Johnny Belinda*

The Treasure of the Sierra Madre

A Foreign Affair

Adventures of Don Juan

BF's Daughter

Casbah

Deep Waters

Green Grass of Wyoming

I Remember Mama

Joan of Arc*

Portrait of Jennie

*Red River**

Saraband for Dead Lovers

Sorry, Wrong Number

The Emperor Waltz*

The Loves of Carmen

The Luck of the Irish

The Naked City

The Snake Pit*

BLOCKBUSTERS

Easter Parade **

The Red Shoes **

Call Northside 777

Cass Timberlane

Homecoming

Oliver Twist

Sitting Pretty

State of the Union

The Babe Ruth Story

The Paleface

The Three Musketeers

CRITICALLY ACCLAIMED

3 Godfathers

Drunken Angel

Germany, Year Zero

Letter from an Unknown Woman

Moonrise

No Orchids for Miss Blandish

Rope

Secret Beyond the Door

The Fallen Idol

The Lady from Shanghai

They Live by Night

Unfaithfully Yours

Your Children's Sleep

DOCUMENTARIES

Louisiana Story

Shadow of the Ruhu

The Secret Land

The Quiet One

Farrebique

The Vatican

Is Everybody Listening

Three Dawns to Sydney

Muscle Beach

HORROR & CULT

Force of Evil

The Dark Past

The Amazing Mr. X

FOREIGN FILMS

Children of the Beehive   JPN

Spring in a Small Town   CH

The Bicycle Thief   IT   **[3]**

The Sunless Street   SPA

ANIMATED SHORT

The Little Orphan

Robin Hoodlum

Mickey and the Seal

Tea for Two Hundred

Mouse Wreckers

The Bear That Got a Peacock's Tail

<u>NOTES</u>

What kinds of movies do you not like to watch? (No judgments!)

1947 AWARD SEASON

Crossfire

Gentleman's Agreement* **[2]**

A Double Life

Black Narcissus

Dark Passage

Great Expectations

Green Dolphin Street*

Kiss of Death

Life with Father*

Miracle on 34th Street

Mourning Becomes Electra

Odd Man Out

Ride the Pink Horse

That Hager Girl

The Bachelor and the Bobby-Soxer*

The Bishop's Wife

The Egg and I*

The Foxes of Harrow

The Ghost and Mrs. Muir

The Search

The Sin of Harold Diddlebock

BLOCKBUSTERS

Forever Amber

Cass Timberlane

Unconquered

It Happened on 5th Avenue

Welcome Stranger

Mother Wore Tights

Road to Rio

California

CRITICALLY ACCLAIMED

Brute Force

Nightmare Alley

Monsieur Verdoux

Out of the Past

DOCUMENTARIES

Design for Death

The World is Rich

Journey Into Medicine

Those Blasted Kids

FOREIGN FILMS

Antoine & Antoinette   FR

Monsieur Vincent   FR

The Damned   FR

Goldsmiths' Quay   FR

Panique   FR

The Ball at the Anjo House   JPN

The Last Stage   POL

The Pearl   MEX

ANIMATED SHORT

Tweetie Pie

Chip an' Dale

Dr. Jekyll and Mr. Mouse

Pluto's Blue Note

Tubby the Tuba

<u>NOTES</u>

Favorite horror film? What's the scariest movie you've ever seen?

1946 AWARD SEASON

The Best Years of Our Lives*   [3]

A Stolen Life

Anna and the King of Siam

Blue Skies*

Canyon Passage

Centennial Summer

Children of Paradise

Duel in the Sun*

Gilda

Henry V

Humoresque

It's a Wonderful Life

Night and Day

*Notorious**

Road to Utopia*

Sister Kenny

The Big Sleep

The Blue Dahlia

The Dark Mirror

The Green Years

The Harvey Girls

The Jolson Story*

The Killers

The Last Chance

The Postman Always Rings Twice

1946

The Razor's Edge*

The Stranger

The Spiral Staircase

The Yearling*

The Strange Love of Martha Ivers

To Each His Own

BLOCKBUSTERS

The Outlaw

Two Years Before the Mast

Till the Clouds Roll By

CRITICALLY ACCLAIMED

Cluny Brown

My Darling Clementine

Great Expectations

Peter and the Wolf

FOREIGN FILMS

Lowly City   IND

Men Without Wings   CZE

Pastoral Symphony   FR

A Matter of Life and Death   UK

Beauty and the Beast   FR

Green For Danger   UK

Paisan   IT

Shoeshine   IT

Utamaro and His Five Women   JPN

ANIMATED SHORT

The Cat Concerto

John Henry and the Inky-Poo

Musical Moments from Chopin

Squatter's Rights

The Bear That Got a Peacock's Tail

Walky Talky Hawky

<u>NOTES</u>

What's the most disturbing movie you've ever watched?

1945 AWARD SEASON

Brief Encounter*

The Bells of St. Mary's*

The Lost Weekend*   [2]

Ziegfeld Follies

A Medal for Benny

A Song to Remember

A Thousand and One Nights

A Tree Grows in Brooklyn

A Walk in the Sun

Anchors Aweigh*

Caesar and Cleopatra

Flame of Barbary Coast

Kitty

Love Letters

Mildred Pierce

Objective, Burma!

San Antonio

Scarlet Street

Spellbound*

State Fair

The Corn is Green

The Dolly Sisters

The Keys of the Kingdom

The Picture of Dorian Gray

The Seventh Veil

The Southerner

The Spiral Staircase

The Story of GI Joe

The Valley of Decision*

They Were Expendable

Tonight and Every Night

Vacation from Marriage

Why Girls Leave Home

BLOCKBUSTERS

Adventure

Leave Her to Heaven

Saratoga Trunk

Son of Lassie

Thrill of a Romance

Week-End at the Waldorf

CRITICALLY ACCLAIMED

Brewster's Millions

Captain Kidd

Dead of Night

Detour

Dillinger

G. I. Honeymoon

Guest in the House

Guest Wife

Hitchhike to Happiness

Incendiary Blonde

Marie Louise

Paris Underground

Pride of the Marines

Rhapsody in Blue

Salty O'Rourke

Sunbonnet Sue

The Affairs of Susan

The Battle of San Pietro

The Enchanted Cottage

The House on 92nd Street

The Man Who Walked Alone

The Woman in the Window

This Love of Ours

What Next, Corporal Hargrove?

Wonder Man

DOCUMENTARIES

The True Glory

The Last Bomb

1945

ANIMATED SHORT

Quiet Please!

Mighty Mouse in Gypsy Life

Donald's Crime

Momotaro, Sacred Sailors   JPN

Jasper and the Beanstalk

Rippling Romance

Life with Feathers

The Poet and Peasant

FOREIGN FILMS

Rome, Open City   IT

Kolberg   GER

The Turning Point   USSR

Ladies of the Bois de Boulogne   FR

A Cage of Nightingales   FR

The Children of Paradise   FR

And Then There Were None   UK

The Last Chance   SWE

Blithe Spirit   UK

The Red Meadows   DNK

I Know Where I'm Going   UK

<u>NOTES</u>

Which movie villain do you most hate (or love to hate)?

1944 AWARD SEASON

Going My Way **[2]**

Belle of the Yukon

Can't Help Singing

Cover Girl

Double Indemnity

Dragon Seed

Gaslight

Hail the Conquering Hero*

Henry V the Fifth

Home in Indiana

Lady in the Dark

Laura*

Lifeboat*

Meet Me in St. Louis*

Mrs. Parkington

Murder, My Sweet
(Farewell My Lovely)

National Velvet

None But the Lonely Heart

Since You Went Away*

The Miracle of Morgan's Creek

The Seventh Cross

The Sullivans

The Three Caballeros

The Uninvited

The White Cliffs of Dover*

Thirty Seconds Over Tokyo*

This Happy Breed

To Have and Have Not*

Two Girls and a Sailor

Wilson

BLOCKBUSTERS

Arsenic and Old Lace

Frenchman's Creek

Ghost Catchers

Hollywood Canteen

I'll Be Seeing You

Up in Arms

Winged Victory

CRITICALLY ACCLAIMED

Address Unknown

Brazil

Casanova Brown

Christmas Holiday

Days of Glory

Higher and Higher

Irish Eyes Are Smiling

It Happened Tomorrow

Jack London

Janie

1944

Knickerbocker Holiday

Lady, Let's Dance

Minstrel Men

Mr. Skeffington

Music For Millions

No Time for Love

None Shall Escape

Secret Command

Sensations of 1945

Song of the Open Road

Step Lively

Summer Storm

The Adventures of Mark Twain

The Bridge of San Luis Rey

The Desert Song

The Fighting Seabees

The Hairy Ape

The Merry Monahans

The Princess and the Pirate

Three Russian Girls

Wing and a Prayer,
The Story of Carrier X

DOCUMENTARIES

The Fighting Lady

Resisting Enemy Interrogation

FOREIGN FILMS

Torment   SWE

Ivan the Terrible ('44 & 58)   USSR

A Canterbury Tale   UK

The Children Are Watching Us   IT

Army   JPN

ANIMATED SHORT

Mouse Trouble

How to Play Football

And to Think That I Saw It
On Mulberry Street

My Boy, Johnny

Dog, Cat and Canary

Swooner Crooner

Fish Fry

<u>NOTES</u>

Who is your favorite screenwriter? What are their best works?

1943 AWARD SEASON

For Whom the Bell Tolls

The Song of Bernadette*

Air Force

Cabin in the Sky

Destination Tokyo*

Five Graves to Cairo

Heaven Can Wait

Hello, Frisco, Hello*

Holy Matrimony

I Walked with a Zombie

In Which We Serve

Madame Curie

Mission to Moscow

Phantom of the Opera

Princess O' Rourke

Sahara

Shadow of a Doubt

So Proudly We Hail!

Stormy Weather

The Amazing Mrs. Holiday

The Constant Nymph

The Human Comedy

The More the Merrier

The North Star

The Ox-Bow Incident

Watch on the Rhine

BLOCKBUSTERS

This is the Army

Hitler's Children

A Guy Named Joe

Mr. Lucky

Coney Island

Stage Door Canteen

Crash Dive

Sweet Rosie O'Grady

Dixie

Thousands Cheer

CRITICALLY ACCLAIMED

Bombardier

Hit Parade of 1943/
Change of Heart

Forever and a Day

In Old Oklahoma

Hangmen Also Die!

Jane Eyre

Her's To Hold

Lady of Burlesque

Hi Diddle Diddle

Lassie Come Home

His Butler's Sister

Riding High

1943

So This is Washington

The Gang's All Here

Something to Shout About

The Kansan

Thank Your Lucky Stars

The Seventh Victim

The Fallen Sparrow

<u>DOCUMENTARIES</u>

Desert Victory

The Battle of Russia

Baptism of Fire

Victory Through Air Power

Report from the Aleutians

War Department Report

FOREIGN FILMS

Portrait of Maria   MEX

The Life and Death of
Colonel Blimp   UK

Day of Wrath   DNK

The Life of Matsu the Untamed
JPN

Fires Were Started   UK

The Man in Grey   UK

Obsession   IT

The Raven   FR

ANIMATED SHORT

The Yankee Doodle Mouse

Reason and Emotion

Greetings Bait!

The 500 Hats of
Bartholomew Cubbins

Imagination

The Dizzy Acrobat

<u>NOTES</u>

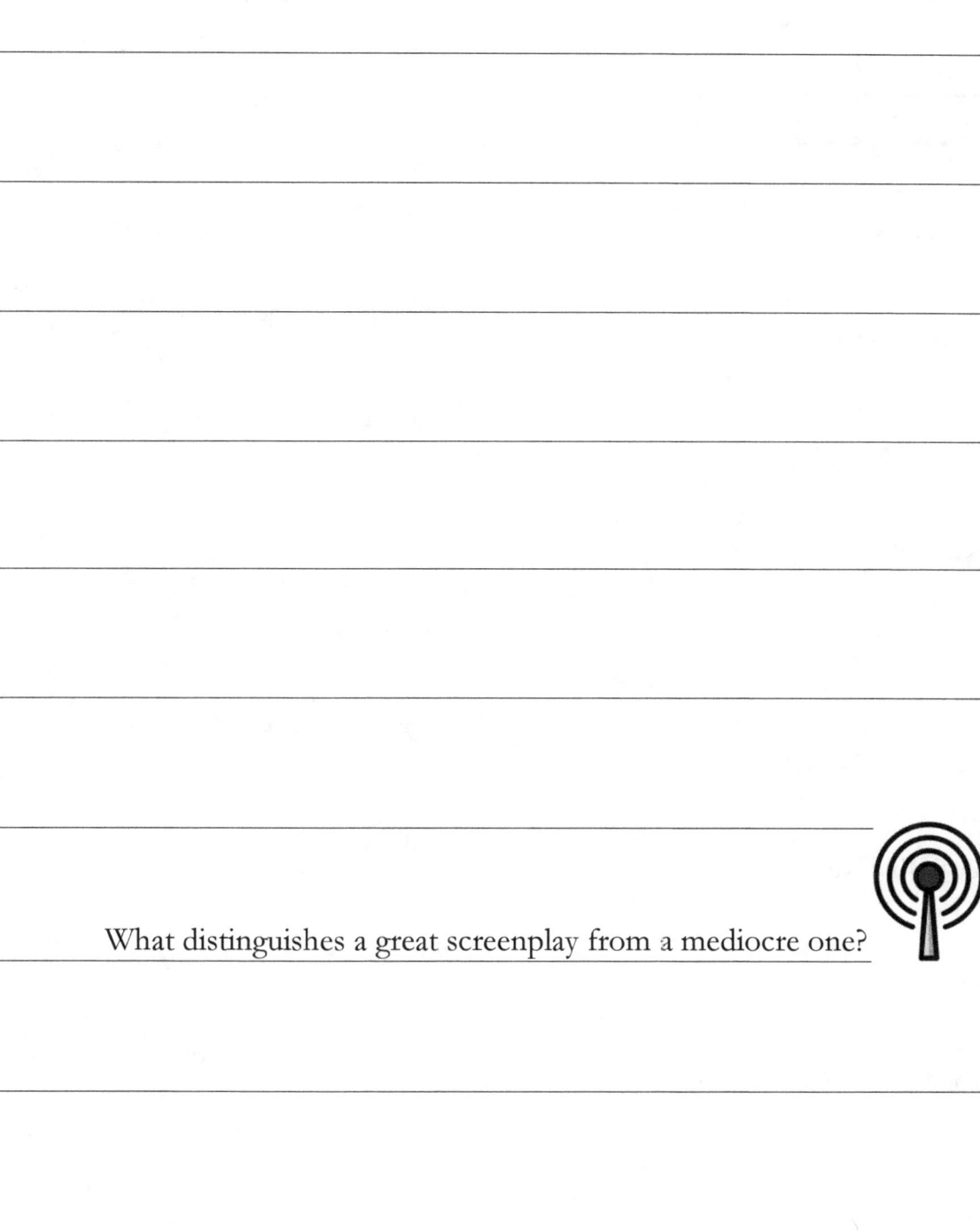

What distinguishes a great screenplay from a mediocre one?

1942 AWARD SEASON

Casablanca

Mrs. Miniver*

Cat People

Gentleman Jim

I Married a Witch

Kings Row

Now, Voyager

Random Harvest*

The Gold Rush

The Invaders

The Magnificent Ambersons

The Man Who Came to Dinner

The Palm Beach Story

The Pied Piper

The Pride of the Yankees*

The Talk of the Town

There Was a Father

This Gun for Hire

To Be or Not to Be

Wake Island*

Woman of the Year

Yankee Doodle Dandy*

BLOCKBUSTERS

Bambi

Somewhere I'll Find You

For Me and My Gal

Springtime in the Rockies

Holiday Inn

Star Spangled Rhythm

Reap the Wild Wind

The Black Swan

Road to Morocco

To the Shores of Tripoli

CRITICALLY ACCLAIMED

Mr. Blabbermouth

The New Spirit

Saludos Amigos

The Price of Victory

Stand by for Action

Twenty-One Miles

The Moon and Sixpence

Winning Your Wings

DOCUMENTARIES

Kokada Front Line!

Conquer by the Clock

Moscow Strikes Back

David Lean Directs Noel Coward

Prelude to War

Henry Browne, Farmer

The Battles of Norway

High Over the Borders

Africa, Prelude to Victory

It's Everybody's War

Citizen of the World: Native Land

The Grain That Built a Hemisphere

Combat Report

FOREIGN FILMS

Four Steps in the Clouds   IT

The War at Sea from Hawaii
to Malaya   JPN

In Which We Serve   UK

ANIMATED SHORT

Der Fuehrer's Face

Juke Box Jamboree

All Out for 'V'

Pigs in a Polka

Blitz Wolf

Tulips Shall Grow

<u>NOTES</u>

Have you ever written a script? What's it about? What's its title?

1941 AWARD SEASON

How Green Was My Valley*

*Citizen Kane**

A Yank in the R.A.F.*

Dive Bomber

All American Co-Ed

Dr. Jekyll and Mr. Hyde

Aloma and the South Seas

Dumbo

Appointment For Love

Flight Command

Back Street

Here Comes Mr. Jordan

Billy the Kid

High Sierra

Birth of the Blues

Hold Back the Dawn

Blood and Sand

I Wanted Wings

Blossoms in the Dust

Ice-Capades

Blues in the Night

King of the Zombies

Buck Privates

Ladies in Retirement

Cheers for Miss Bishop

Las Vegas Nights

1941

Louisiana Purchase*	That Uncertain Feeling
Lydia	The Chocolate Soldier
Mercy Island	*The Devil and Daniel Webster*
Night Train to Munich	The Devil and Miss Jones
One Foot in Heaven	The Devil Pays Off
Penny Serenade	The Flame of New Orleans
Ridin' on a Rainbow	The Great Lie
Skylark	The Invisible Woman
So Ends Our Night	The Lady Eve
Sundown	The Little Foxes*
Suspicion	The Maltese Falcon
Tall, Dark and Handsome	The Men in Her Life
Tanks a Million	The Sea Wolf
That Hamilton Woman	The Strawberry Blonde

1941

The Wolf Man

Topper Returns

This Woman is Mine

You'll Never Ger Rich

Tom, Dick and Harry

BLOCKBUSTERS

Sergeant York **

In the Navy

Babes on Broadway

Meet John Doe

Ball of Fire*

Men of Boys Town

Caught in the Draft

Road to Zanzibar

Charley's Aunt

Sun Valley Serenade

Honky Tonk

DOCUMENTARIES

Churchill's Island

A Letter from Home

A Place to Live

Adventure in the Bronx

Bomber: A Defense Report on Film

Christmas Under Fire

Kukan

Life of a Thoroughbred

Norway in Revolt

Russian Soil

Soldiers of the Sky

Target for Tonight

Warclouds

ANIMATED SHORT

Lend a Paw

Boogie Woogie Bugle Boy
of Company B

Hiawatha's Rabbit Hunt

How War Came

Rhapsody in Rivets

Rhythm in the Ranks

Superman

The Night Before Christmas

The Rookie Bear

Truant Officer Donald

FOREIGN FILMS

Ornamental Hairpin   JPN

HONORABLE MENTION

49th Parallel   Never Give a Sucker an Even Break

All That Money Can Buy   Sis Hopkins

Hellzapoppin'   Sullivan's Travels

Johnny Eager   The Son of Monte Cristo

Man Hunt   The White Eagle

Mr. & Mrs. Smith   When Ladies Meet

<u>NOTES</u>

Who do you usually watch movies with?

1940 AWARD SEASON

Rebecca

All This, and Heaven Too

Angels Over Broadway

Comrade X

Dark Command

Dr. Ehrlick's Magic Bullet

Edison, The Man

Foreign Correspondent

His Girl Friday

Kitty Foyle

My Favorite Wife

Our Town

Primrose Path

Second Chorus

Strike Up the Band*

The Fight for Life

The Grapes of Wrath

The Great Dictator

The House of the Seven Gables

The Letter

The Long Voyage Home

The Philadelphia Story

The Westerner

They Knew What They Wanted

BLOCKBUSTERS

Boom Town

One Million BC

Pinocchio **

Pride and Prejudice

Andy Hardy Meets Debutante

Santa Fe Trail

Arise, My Love

The Blue Bird

Down Argentine Way

The Fighting 69th

Fantasia

The Mark of Zorro

Hit Parade of 1941

The Sea Hawk

Irene

The Shop Around the Corner

North West Mounted Police

Tin Pan Alley

Northwest Passage

CRITICALLY ACCLAIMED

Abe Lincoln in Illinois

The Bank Dick

Arizona

The Great McGinty

Behind the News

The Howards of Virginia

Captain Caution

The Mortal Storm

Dance, Girl, Dance

The Thief of Bagdad

Knute Rockne: All American

Waterloo Bridge

Rhythm on the River

You'll Find Out

Spring on Leper's Island   JPN

DOCUMENTARIES

Citizen of the World: The Proud Valley

Night Train to Munich

ANIMATED SHORT

The Milky Way   Puss Gets the Boot

A Wild Hare

HONORABLE MENTION

Bitter Sweet   The Boys from Syracuse

Dr. Cyclops   The Invisible Man Returns

Lillian Russell   Too Many Husbands

Music In My Heart   Typhoon

My Son! My Son!   Women in War

Swiss Family Robinson

<u>NOTES</u>

What's the most unexpected plot twist you've seen in a movie?

1939 AWARD SEASON

Gone with the Wind

Union Pacific

Babes in Arms*

Bachelor Mother

Balalaika

Beau Geste

Captain Fury

Dark Victory

Drums Along the Mohawk

Eternally Yours

First Love

Golden Boy

Goodbye, Mr. Chips

Intermezzo

Juarez

Love Affair

Man of Conquest

Mr. Smith Goes to Washington*

Ninotchka

Nurse Edith Cavell

Of Mice and Men

Second Fiddle

She Married a Cop

Stagecoach

Swanee River

The Great Victor Herbert

1939

The Hunchback of Notre Dame*

The Man in the Iron Mask

The Private Lives of
Elizabeth and Essex

The Rains Came

The Wizard of Oz*

They Shall Have Music

Way Down South

When Tomorrow Comes

Wuthering Heights

Young Mr. Lincoln

BLOCKBUSTERS

Dodge City

Gunga Din

Jesse James

CRITICALLY ACCLAIMED

Destry Rides Again

The Cat and the Canary

Gulliver's Travels

The Four Feathers

Lying Lips

The Mikado

Only Angels Have Wings

The Roaring Twenties

Peace on Earth

The Women

FOREIGN FILMS

Christian   CZE

The Rules of the Game   FR

Daybreak   FR

The Story of the Late Chrysanthemums
JPN

<u>NOTES</u>

Do you watch independent films?

1938 AWARD SEASON

You Can't Take It With You*

Alexander's Ragtime Band*

Algiers

Angels With Dirty Faces

Army Girl

Blockade

Block-Heads

Boys Town*

Breaking the Ice

Carefree

Four Daughters

Girls' School

Going Places

Grand Illusion

Holiday

If I Were King*

In Old Chicago*

Jezebel

Mad About Music

Of Human Hearts

Pygmalion

Storm Over Bengal

Suez

Test Pilot*

The Adventures of Robin Hood*

The Buccaneer

The Citadel

The Young in Heart

The Cowboy and the Lady

There Goes My Heart

The Goldwyn Follies

Tropic Holiday

The Great Waltz

BLOCKBUSTERS

Snow White and the
Seven Dwarfs

Sweethearts

The Adventures of Marco Polo

Love Finds Andy Hardy

The Terror of Tiny Town

Marie Antoinette

CRITICALLY ACCLAIMED

Alexander Nevsky

Pacific Liner

Bringing Up Baby

Port of Shadows

Kentucky

The Dawn Patrol

Merrily We Live

The Lady Objects

1938

The Lady Vanishes

Vivacious Lady

Three Comrades

White Banners

Under Western Stars

ANIMATED SHORT

Ferdinand the Bull

Hunky and Spunky

Brave Little Tailor

Mother Goose Goes Hollywood

Good Scouts

FOREIGN FILMS

Fallen Blossoms   JPN

The Baker's Wife   FR

Hotel Du Nord   FR

The Human Beast
Judas Was a Woman   FR

<u>NOTES</u>

Have you ever attended a film festival?
Which one would you go to?

1937 AWARD SEASON

<mark>The Life of Emile Zola</mark>

A Star Is Born*

Artists and Models

Captains Courageous*

Conquest*

Dead End*

Grand Illusion

Hitting a New High*

Lost Horizon*

Make a Wish*

Mannequin

Maytime*

Mr. Dodd Takes the Air*

Night Must Fall*

One Hundred Men and a Girl

Portia on Trial*

Quality Street*

Something to Sing About*

Stage Door

Stella Dallas*

The Awful Truth

The Girl Said No*

The Good Earth*

The Prisoner of Zenda*

Walter Wagner's Vogues of 1938*

Way Out West*

<u>BLOCKBUSTERS</u>

Saratoga

A Day at the Races

Black Legion

Broadway Melody of 1938

Every Day's a Holiday

Manhattan Merry-Go-Round

Ready, Willing and Able

Shall We Dance

Souls at Sea

Thin Ice

Topper

Variety Show

Waikiki Wedding

Wee Willie Winkie

Wells Fargo

Wings Over Honolulu

You're a Sweetheart

CRITICALLY ACCLAIMED

History is Made at Night

Pepe Le Moko

Humanity and Paper Balloons

Pioneer: Jericho

Make Way for Tomorrow

The Tale of the Fox

<u>NOTES</u>

Do you like black & white classics?

1936 AWARD SEASON

San Francisco*

The Great Ziegfeld*

A Tale of Two Cities

Anthony Adverse*

Banjo on My Knee

Born to Dance

Cain and Mabel

Come and Get It

Dancing Pirate

Dodsworth

General Spanky

King of Burlesque

Libeled Lady*

Lloyds of London*

Magnificent Brute

Mr. Deeds Goes to Town

One in a Million

Pennies from Heaven

Pigskin Parade

Romeo and Juliet

Sing, Baby, Sing

Suzy

Swing Time*

BLOCKBUSTERS

After the Thin Man

Strike Me Pink

Modern Times

The Last of the Mohicans

Rose Marie

The Plainsman

FOREIGN FILMS

A Day in the Country FR

Sisters of the Gion JPN

Cesar FR

Two Films by Yasujiro Ozu JPN
- *The Only Son*

Redes MEX

- *There Was a Father*

CRITICALLY ACCLAIMED

Camille

The Lower Depths ('36 &57)

My Man Godfrey

The Only Son

Reefer Madness

The Story of a Cheat

Sabotage

Theodora Goes Wild

Showboat

These Three

Things to Come

Valiant is the Word for Carrie

Trail of the Lonesome Pine

<u>NOTES</u>

What book-to-movie adaptation impressed you?
Which one disappointed you?

1935 AWARD SEASON

Mutiny on the Bounty

$1,000 a Minute

A Midsummer Night's Dream

Alice Adams

Barbary Coast

Becky Sharp

Black Fury

Captain Blood

Dangerous

David Copperfield*

Escape Me Never

Folies Bergere de Paris

G Men

Go Into Your Dance

I Dream Too Much

Les Misérables

Love Me Forever*

Naughty Marietta

Peter Ibbetson

Private Worlds

Ruggles of Red Gap

She

The Informer

The Lives of a Bengal Lancer*

The Scoundrel

1935

BLOCKBUSTERS

Broadway Melody of 1936

Steamboat Round the Bend

China Seas

The Crusades

Roberta

Top Hat

CRITICALLY ACCLAIMED

A Night at the Opera

The 39 Steps

Bride of Frankenstein

The Devil is a Woman

Dandy Dick

The Raven

In Old Kentucky

Toni

DOCUMENTARIES

After the Thin Man	San Francisco
Anthony Adverse	Strike Me Pink
Libeled Lady	Swing Time
Modern Times	The Great Ziegfeld
Pioneer: Sanders of the River	The Plainsman
Rose Marie	

FOREIGN FILMS

Let's Go with Pancho Villa MEX	Wife! Be Like a Rose! JPN

NOTES

Who is your favorite director? What are their best films?

1934 AWARD SEASON

It Happened One Night

Cleopatra

Flirtation Walk

Here Comes the Navy

Hide-Out

Imitation of Life

Manhattan Melodrama

One Night of Love

Operator 13

She Loves Me Not

The Affairs of Cellini

The Barretts of Wimpole Street

The Gay Divorcee

The House of Rothschild

The Lost Patrol

The Richest Girl in the World

The Thin Man

The White Parade

Viva Villa!

BLOCKBUSTERS

Babes in Toyland

Stand Up and Cheer!

Bright Eyes

The Black Cat

It's a Gift

The Scarlett Empress

Little Miss Marker

Triumph of the Will

Maniac

FOREIGN FILMS

Our Neighbour, Miss Yae   JPN

The Passing Barge   FR

The Goddess   CH

Two Monks   MEX

<u>NOTES</u>

If you were a movie director,
what genre would your debut film belong to?

1933 AWARD SEASON

Cavalcade

Morning Glory

42nd Street*

Reunion in Vienna

Berkeley Square

She Done Him Wrong*

Eskimo

Sons of the Desert

Flying Down to Rio

State Fair*

Lady for a Day

The Private Life of Henry VIII

Little Women*

When Ladies Meet

BLOCKBUSTERS

I'm No Angel

Dinner at Eight

King Kong

Footlight Parade

Roman Scandals

Gold Diggers of 1933

Dancing Lady

Tugboat Annie

CRITICALLY ACCLAIMED

Alice in Wonderland

The Bitter Tea of General Yen

Desire for Living

The Emperor Jones

Land Without Bread

The Story of Temple Drake

Queen Christina

Zero for Conduct

FOREIGN FILMS

Japanese Girls at the Harbour   JPN

*The Testament /
Last Will of Dr. Mabuse*   GER

Outskirts   USSR

1933

<u>NOTES</u>

Is there a film you disliked initially but grew to love over time?

1932 AWARD SEASON

Grand Hotel*

A Farewell to Arms

I Am a Fugitive from a Chain Gang

Lady and Gent

Love Me Tonight

One Hour with You*

One Way Passage

Scarface: The Shame of a Nation

Shanghai Express

Smilin' Through*

What Price Hollywood?

BLOCKBUSTERS

The Kid from Spain

The Sign of the Cross

As You Desire Me

Bring 'Em Back Alive

Emma

Hell Divers

Movie Crazy

Prosperity

Strange Interlude

Tarzan the Ape Man

CRITICALLY ACCLAIMED

Blonde Venus

Merrily We Go to Hell

Trouble in Paradise

Rasputin and the Empress

FOREIGN FILMS

Boudu Saved from Drowning   FR

Fanny   FR

I Was Born, but…   JPN

Vampyr   GER/FR

HORROR & CULT

Doctor X

Freaks

Island of Lost Souls

The Mask of Fu Manchu

The Most Dangerous Game

White Zombie

<u>NOTES</u>

What's your favorite decade or era of filmmaking?

1931 AWARD SEASON

Cimarron*

A Free Soul

Arrowsmith*

Bad Girl*

East Lynne

Five Star Final

Ships of Hate

Skippy

Tabu

The Champ

The Front Page

The Sin of Madelon Claudet

The Smiling Lieutenant

Transatlantic

BLOCKBUSTERS

City Lights

A Connecticut Yankee

Merely Mary Ann

Palmy Days

The Man Who Came Back

Trader Horn

CRITICALLY ACCLAIMED

Dishonored

Little Caesar

Madchen in Uniform

Night Nurse

The Guardsman

The Public Enemy

ANIMATED SHORT

Mickey's Orphans

FOREIGN FILMS

Comradeship   FR/GER

Freedom for US   FR

Limite   BRZ

M   GER

Marius   FR

The Bitch FR

The Million   FR

The Neighbour's Wife and Mine JPN

The Threepenny Opera   GER

HORROR & CULT

Daddy Long Legs

Frankenstein

Dr. Jekyll and Mr. Hyde

Hell Divers

Dracula

<u>NOTES</u>

What's the best documentary you've ever seen?

1930 AWARD SEASON

All Quiet on the Western Front

Anna Christie

Holiday

King of Jazz

Min and Bill*

Raffles

Sarah and Son

Street of Chance

The Age of Gold

The Big Pond

The Big Trail

The Case of Sgt. Grischa

The Divorcee

The Green Goddess

The Love Parade

The Rogue Son

With Byrd at the South Pole

BLOCKBUSTERS

Whoopee! **

Hold Everything

Animal Crackers

Morocco

Check and Double Check

Son of the Gods

Common Clay

Song o' My Heart

Hell's Angels

The Big House

FOREIGN FILMS

Earth   SOV

The Orphic Trilogy 1:
The Blood of a Poet   FR

Goodbye Argentina   ARG

Under the Roofs of Paris   FR

People on Sunday   FR

Westfront 1918   GER

The Blue Angel   GER

What Made Her Do It?   JPN

<u>NOTES</u>

What movie has been on your watchlist for a long time?

FILMS OF 1929

The Broadway Melody

Alibi

Blackmail

Bulldog Drummond

Coquette

Disraeli

Drag

Gold Diggers of Broadway

Hallelujah

Hollywood Revue

In Old Arizona

On with the Show!

Rio Rita

Say it with Songs

Sunny Side Up

The Cock-Eyed World

The Desert Song

The Divine Lady

The Last of Mrs. Cheyney

The Leatherneck

The Man with the Movie Camera

The Patriot

The Trespasser

The Valiant

Their Own Desire

Weary River

Welcome Danger

1929

<u>NOTES</u>

In your opinion, what underrated movie should more people watch? **!!**

FILMS OF 1928

The Singing Fool	Sadie Thompson
4 Devils	Sal of Singapore
A Ship Comes In	Skyscraper
A Woman of Affairs	Steamboat Bill Jr.
Eliso	Storm Over Asia
Four Sons	Street Angel
Lights of New York	The Awakening
Lonesome	*The Cameraman*
My Man	*The Circus*
Noah's Ark	The Cop
On Trial	The Crowd
Our Dancing Daughters	The Docks of New York
Plane Crazy	*The Last Command*

1928

The Noose

The Red Dance

The Road to Ruin

The Terror

White Shadows in the South Seas

FOREIGN FILMS

A Throw of Dice   IND

An Andalusian Dog   FR

Crossroads   JPN

Days of Youth   JPN

Pandora's Box   GER

The Passion of Joan of Arc   FR

<u>NOTES</u>

What movie would you say deserves a sequel (or prequel)?

FILMS OF 1927

Wings

7th Heaven

A Diary of Chuji's Travels

Chang

Don Juan

London After Midnight

Metropolis

Napoleon

October

Sunrise: A Song of Two Humans

The Devil Dancer

The Dove

The General

The Jazz Singer

The Kid Brother

The King of Kings

The Lodger:
A Story of the London Fog

The Magic Flame

The Patent Leather Kid

The Racket

The Unknown

The Way of All Flesh

Two Arabian Knights

Underworld

When a Man Loves

<u>NOTES</u>

Imagine a crossover between two of your favorite movies.
How would the story unfold?

FILMS OF 1926

What Price Glory?

3 Bad Men

A Page of Madness   JPN

Beau Geste

Don Juan

Flesh and the Devil

For Heaven's Sake

Menilmontant

Oh! What a Nurse!

Old Ironsides

Private Izzy Murphy

Tell It to the Marines

The Adventures of Prince Achmed
GER

The Better Ole

The Black Pirate

The Cohens and Kellys

The General

The Sea Beast

The Son of the Sheik

<u>NOTES</u>

Describe a movie that changed your Life.

FILMS OF 1925

The Big Parade

Battleship Potemkin

Ben-Hur: A Tale of the Christ

Charley's Aunt

Don Q, Son of Zorro

East Lynne

Little Annie Rooney

Madame Sans Gene

Orochi   JPN

Seven Chances

Stella Dallas

The Eagle

The Freshman

The Gold Rush

The Great Divide

The Lost World

The Merry Widow

The Phantom of the Opera

DOCUMENTARIES

Borderline

Master of the House

Outsider: Body and Soul

Paul Robeson: Portraits of the Artist (1925-79)

<u>NOTES</u>

Has a movie ever changed your perspective on a certain topic?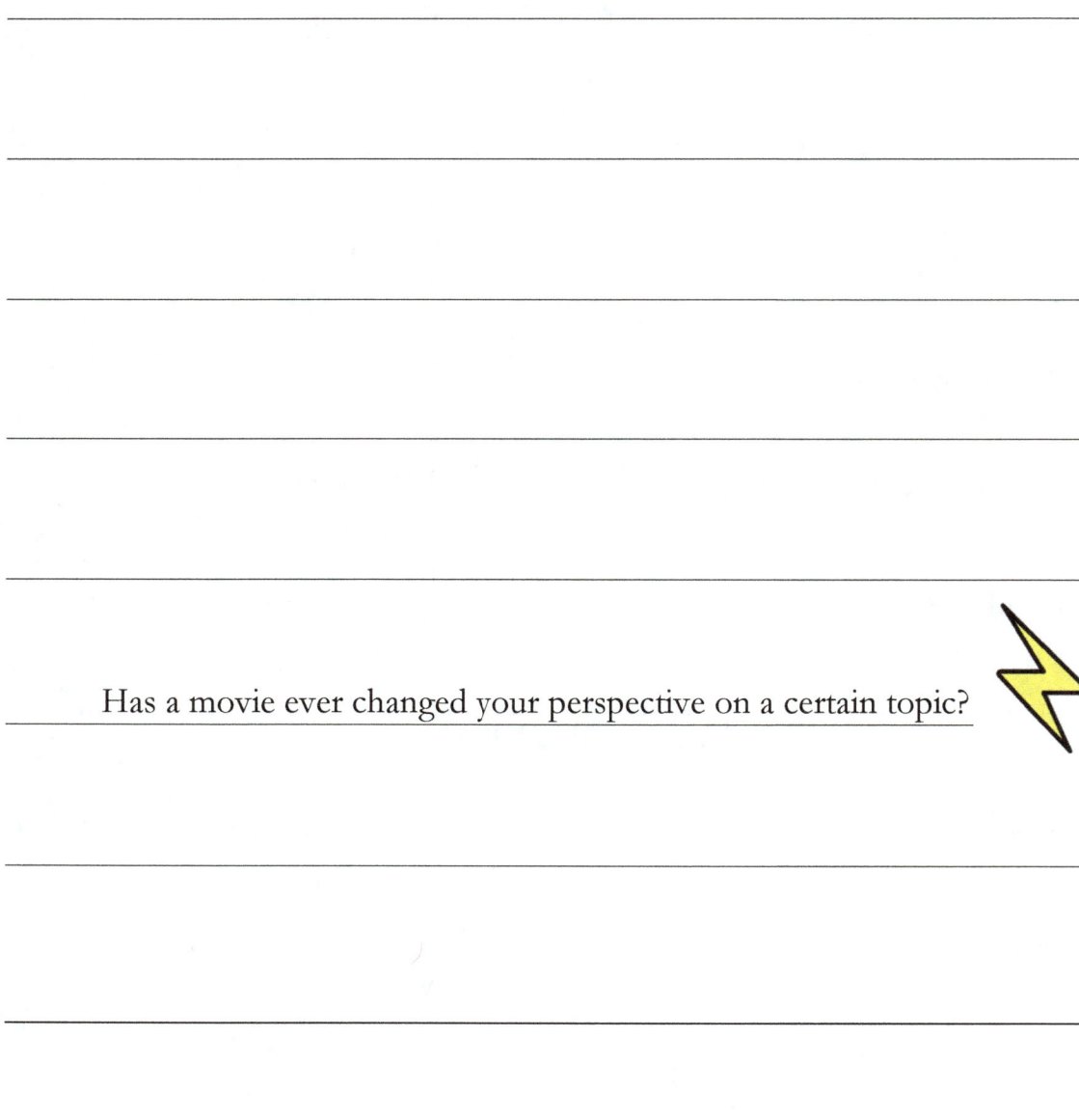

FILMS OF 1924

The Sea Hawk

A Society Scandal

Beau Brummel

Entr'acte

Girl Shy

He Who Gets Slapped

His Hour

Hot Water

Monsieur Beaucaire

Secrets

Sherlock Jr.

Strike

The Dixie Handicap

The Great White Silence

The Humming Bird

The Inhuman Woman

The Iron Horse

The Last Laugh

The Marriage Circle

The Thief of Bagdad

<u>NOTES</u>

What's the very first film you remember seeing at the movies?

FILMS OF 1923

The Covered Wagon

A Woman of Paris: A Drama of Fate

Adam's Rib

Brass

Daddy

Homeward Bound

Little Old New York

Main Street

Our Hospitality

Safety Last!

Scaramouche

The Gold Diggers

The Hunchback of Notre Dame

The Ne'er-Do-Well

The Pilgrim

The Ten Commandments

The White Sister

Tiger Rose

Where the North Begins

<u>NOTES</u>

Top 5!! Write down five film recommendations

FILMS OF 1922

Blood and Sand

Dr. Mabuse, the Gambler

Foolish Wives

Manslaughter

Nosferatu, A Symphony of Terror

Oliver Twist

Smilin' Through

When Knighthood Was in Flower

BLOCKBUSTERS

Robin Hood

A Dangerous Adventure

Blood and Sand

Grandma's Boy

Heroes of the Street

Rags to Riches

The Beautiful and Damned

Your Best Friend

DOCUMENTARIES

Haxan: Witchcraft Through the Ages

Nanook of the North

The Smiling Madame Beudet

<u>NOTES</u>

What movie has stayed with you long after watching it?

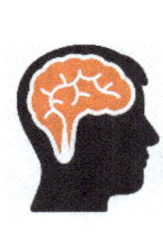

FILMS OF 1921

The Four Horsemen of
The Apocalypse

Brewster's Millions

Little Lord Fauntleroy

Orphans of the Storm

School Days

The Kid

The Love Light

The Passion Flower

The Phantom Carriage

The Sheik

The Three Musketeers

White and Unmarried

Why Girls Leave Home

<u>NOTES</u>

What upcoming movie(s) are you most looking forward to?

FILMS OF 1920

Way Down East

Double Speed

Dr. Jekyll and Mr. Hyde

Excuse My Dust

Over the Hill to the Poorhouse

Pollyanna

Shipwrecked Among Cannibals

Something to Think About

The Cabinet of Dr. Caligari

The Mark of Zorro

The Phantom Carriage

The Round-Up

Within Our Gates

<u>NOTES</u>

What will the movie industry look like 100 years from now?

FILMS OF 1919

Passion: Madame Duberry

The Miracle Man

Broken Blossoms

Daddy Long Legs

Felix the Cat

Hawthorne of the USA

Male and Female

The Homesteader

The Roaring Road

When the Clouds Roll By

NOTES

FILMS OF 1918

Mickey

Stella Maris

Bound in Morocco

Tarzan of the Apes

Headin' South

The Ghost of Slumber Mountain

Old Wives for New

The Squaw Man

Shoulder Arms

The Whispering Chorus

1918

<u>NOTES</u>

FILMS OF 1917

Cleopatra

A Romance of the Redwoods

Mothers of Man

Rebecca of Sunnybrook Farm

The Devil-Stone

The Little America

The Poor Little Rich Girl

The Woman God Forgot

<u>NOTES</u>

FILMS OF 1916

Intolerance

20,000 Leagues Under the Sea

A Grid-Iron Hero

Hulda from Holland

Joan the Woman

Maria Rosa

The Dream Girl

The Heart of Nora Flynn

The Innocent Lie

The Trail of the Lonesome Pine

NOTES

FILMS OF 1915

The Birth of a Nation

Carmen

Chimmie Fadden

Chimmie Fadden Out West

Inspiration

Les Vampires

Temptation

The Arab

The Cheat

The Girl of the Golden West

The Golden Chance

The Warrens of Virginia

WC Fields: Six Short Films

1915

NOTES

FILMS OF 1914

Dough and Dynamite

The Million Dollar Mystery

Rose of the Rancho

The Spoilers

The Call of the North

The Squaw Man

The Man from Home

What's His Name

FILMS OF 1913

A Slave of Satan

Traffic in Souls

<u>NOTES</u>

FILMS OF 1910

A Christmas Carol

Am Abend   GER

As It Is In Life

Cagliostro   FR

Dorian Gray's Portrait   DNK

Frankenstein

The Defeat of Satan   FR

The Fugitive

The Funeral of Edward VII

The Johnson-Jeffries Flight

The White Slave Trade   DNK

NOTES

FILMS BEFORE 1910

Passage de Venus (1874)

Roundhay Garden Scene (1888)

Monkeyshines (1889-90)

Pope Leo XIII (1890s)

Dickson Greeting/Monkeyshines 2 (1891)

Un Bon Bock (1892)

Dickson Experimental Sound Film (1894-95)

Dorlita in the Passion Dance (1894)

The Boxing Cats (1894)

Incident at Clovelly Cottage (1895)

Leaving the Factory (1895)

The Arrest of a Pickpocket (1895)

The Execution of Mary, Queen of Scots (1895)

The Cabbage Fairy (1896)

The Coronation of Tsar Nicholas II (1896)

The House of the Devil (1896)

The Kiss (1896)

After the Ball, the Bath (1897)

Santa Claus (1898)

King John (1899)

The Humpty Dumpty Circus (1899)

Sherlock Holmes Baffled (1900)

Scrooge or Marley's Ghost (1901)

A Trip To The Moon (1902)

Burnley v Manchester United (1902)

The Great Train Robbery (1903)

NOTES

MY FAVORITE FILMS

MY FAVORITE FILMS

MY FAVORITE FILMS

NOTES

NOTES

NOTES

REFERENCES

Antonia, Astrid. "10 Amazing Anime Movies of 2017". Scene 360. 8 Feb 2017: https://scene360.com/movies/104116/amazing-anime-movies-2017/

Archbold, Phil and Brian Boone. "The Worst Movies of 2022". Looper. 6 Jan 2023: https://www.looper.com/752013/worst-movies-2022/

Arto-Karhunen, IMDB contributor. "Top 500 - Greatest Movies of All Time!". The Internet Movie Database. 25 Oct 2012: https://www.imdb.com/list/ls050782187/

Bailey, Jason. "The Best Made for TV Movies of All Time". Flavorwire. 7 Feb 2012: https://www.flavorwire.com/257437/the-best-made-for-tv-movies-of-all-time

Bancroft, Jason. "The Worst Movies of 2022". Ranker. 23 Jan 2024: https://www.ranker.com/list/worst-movies-2022/jason-bancroft

Box Office Mojo contributors. "Domestic Yearly Box Office". Box Office Mojo. https://www.boxofficemojo.com/year/

Calhoun, Dave, Joshua Rothkopf and Time Out contributors. "The 100 Best Animated Movies Ever Made". Time Out New York. 29 Mar 2016: https://www.timeout.com/newyork/film/the-100-best-animated-movies

Campos, Manuel. "100 Questions about Movies for the ESL Classroom". Gather Lessons. 9 Jan 2024: https://gatherlessons.com/questions-about-movies/

Casano, Ann. "The Most Important 'Firsts' in Film History". Ranker, Rankings About Everything. 20 May 2020: https://www.ranker.com/list/cool-film-firsts/anncasano

Childress, Erik and RT Staff. "The 50 Highest-Grossing Movies of All Time: Your Top Box Office Earners Ever Worldwide". Rotten Tomatoes. 12 Aug 2022: https://editorial.rottentomatoes.com/article/highest-grossing-movies-all-time/

CineAutoctono, IMDB contributor. "The Worst Movies of 2022". The Internet Movie Database. 1 Jan 2023: https://www.imdb.com/list/ls519670619/

Classicactresses. IMDB Contributor. "Best Lifetime Movies Ever". The Internet Movie Database. 17 June 2016: https://www.imdb.com/list/ls063569347/

Cook, Meghan. "11 of the Best and 11 of the Worst Movies of the Year, So Far". Business Insider. 30 Dec 2022: https://www.insider.com/best-and-worst-movies-of-2022-critic-ranking

Criterion Collection contributors. "Shop All Films." Criterion Collection. https://www.criterion.com/shop/browse/list

Daniel, Alex. "30 Movie Facts That Will Blow Your Mind". Best Life. 7 Jun 2018: https://bestlifeonline.com/movie-facts/

Dietz, Jason. "The 25 Best Movies of 2023". Metacritic. 4 Jan 2024: https://www.metacritic.com/pictures/best-movies-of-2023/

Dormerjam-1. IMDB Contributor. "Best 48 Made For TV Movies." The Internet Movie Database. 23 Feb 2020: https://www.imdb.com/list/ls032600015/

Ebiri, Bilge, Jovanka Vuckovic and Sam Zimmerman. "10 Best Horror Movies of 2015". Rolling Stone. 23 Dec 2015: www.rollingstone.com/tv-movies/tv-movie-lists/10-best-horror-movies-of-2015-38675/

Eisenbeis, Richard. "The Five Best Anime of 2015". Koratu. 1 Jan 2016: https://kotaku.com/the-five-best-anime-of-2015-1750056677

Eiss, Jennifer, JP Rutter and Steve White. 500 Essential Cult Movies: The Ultimate Guide. Sterling. Aug. 2010.

Fandom contributors. "1,001 Movies You Must See Before You Die". Fandom, Wikia. https://1001films.fandom.com/wiki/The_List

Filmsite contributors. "The Best Movies in Cinematic History Part 1". Filmsite, Greatest Films. https://www.filmsite.org/films.html

Frater, Jamie. "Top 10 Incredible Early Film Firsts". Listverse. 14 Oct 2007: https://listverse.com/2007/10/14/top-10-incredible-early-film-firsts/

Garcia, John David. "10 Monumental Moments in Movie History". Listverse. 27 Sept 2014: https://listverse.com/2014/09/27/10-monumental-milestones-in-movie-history/

Gleiberman, Owen. "1990's Best (and Worst) Movies". Entertainment Weekly. 28 Dec 1990: https://ew.com/article/1990/12/28/1990s-best-and-worst-movies/

Green, Anna. "36 Film History Firsts". Mental Floss. 5 Jan 2016: https://www.mentalfloss.com/article/72060/36-film-history-firsts

Greenwald, Amanda. "The Best Lifetime Movies of All Time". BestLife Online. 25 Oct 2019: https://bestlifeonline.com/best-lifetime-movies

Heggeness, Greta. "The 18 Best Lifetime Movies of All Time". PureWow Online. 1 Nov 2019: https://www.purewow.com/entertainment/best-lifetime-movies

Hermiecabral, IMDB contributor. "Film Firsts". The Internet Movie Database. 4 June 2015: https://www.imdb.com/list/ls072800621/?ref_=rltls_2

IGN Staff. "Best Anime of 2018". IGN. 10 Dec 2018. Web. 21 Dec 2018: https://www.ign.com/articles/2018/12/10/best-anime-movie-2018

IGN Staff and Matt Fowler. "The Worst Reviewed Movies 2021 So Far". IGN. 25 Apr 2021: https://www.ign.com/articles/the-worst-movies-of-2021

Janes, DeAnna. "12 of the Best Lifetime Movies to Record on Your DVR". Oprah Daily. 12 Aug 2019: https://www.oprahdaily.com/entertainment/tv-movies/g28669983/best-lifetime-movies/

Khal, Victoria Johnson. "The Best Black Movies of the Last 30 Years". Complex Magazine. 6 May 2020: https://www.complex.com/pop-culture/the-best-black-movies-of-the-last-30-years/

Lewis, Anna and Emily Gull. "56 of the best Christmas Films of All Time". Cosmopolitan. 26 Oct 2020: https://www.cosmopolitan.com/uk/entertainment/g12156866/best-christmas-films/?slide=1

Lifetime contributors. "11 Movies That Are So 'Wrong' They're Right". Lifetime: https://www.mylifetime.com/11-movies-that-are-so-wrong-theyre-right

Lindwasser, Anna. "The Best Fall 2018 Anime That You Should Be Watching". Ranker. 2 Oct 2018: https://www.ranker.com/list/best-fall-2018-anime/anna-lindwasser?ref=nxtlst&collectionId=2671&li_source=LI&li_medium=desktop-next-list

Lindwasser, Anna. "The 15 Best Anime Movies of 2018 You Don't Want to Miss". Ranker. 7 Oct 2019: https://www.ranker.com/list/best-anime-movies-2018/anna-lindwasser

MACE0204, IMDB contributor. "Top 100 Films of The 50's". The Internet Movie Database. 2 Apr 2011: https://www.imdb.com/list/ls000718198/

MCFJR42, IMDB contributor. "Empire's 500 Greatest Movies of All Time". The Internet Movie Database. 21 Aug 2011: https://www.imdb.com/list/ls003073623 /

MovieBB, IMDB contributor. "IMDB 100 Must-See African-American Films Made". The Internet Movie Database: https://www.listchallenges.com/100-must-see-african-american-films

NG_480, IMDB contributor. "IMDB NC-17 and/or X Rated Films". The Internet Movie Database. 11 Aug 2011: https://www.imdb.com/list/ls007387528/

Nichols, Peter M, editor. The New York Times - The Best DVDs You've Never Seen, Just Missed or Almost Forgotten. St. Martin's Griffin. 2005.

Pooley, Jack. "20 Worst Movies of 2022". What Culture. 3 Jun 2022: https://whatculture.com/film/20-worst-movies-of-2022-so-far

Oken, Ashley. "These Black History Documentaries Will Help You Expand Your Knowledge and Become a Better Ally". Cosmopolitan. 10 Aug 2020: https://www.cosmopolitan.com/entertainment/movies/a33537429/black-history-documentaries/

Ranker Community contributors. "The Best Black Movies Ever Made, Ranked". Ranker, Rankings About Everything. https://www.ranker.com/crowdranked-list/all-black-movies-or-list-of-black-movies

Ranker Film contributors. "The Best Black and White Movies Ever Made". Ranker, Rankings About Everything. https://www.ranker.com/list/best-black-and-white-movies-ever-made/ranker-film

Ranker Film contributors. "The Most Inspirational Black Movies - Ranker Film". Ranker, Rankings About Everything. https://www.ranker.com/list/inspirational-black-movies/ranker-film?ref=collections&l=612336&collectionId=65

Roberts, Kayleigh. "This Is the First Sex Scene in Movie History". Marie Claire. 15 Mar. 2017: https://www.marieclaire.com/celebrity/news/a25836/first-sex-scene-movie-history/

Roemer, Christian. "5 Fun VHS Facts That Will Blow Your Mind". Analog: A Legacybox Blog. https://legacybox.com/blogs/analog/5-fun-vhs-facts-will-blow-mind

Rosa, Christopher. "The 21 Best Lifetime Movies for When You Need a Total Escape". Glamour. 30 July 2020: https://www.glamour.com/gallery/best-lifetime-movies

Rose, Lily. "The Worst Movies of 2021". CBS News. 22 July 2021: https://www.cbsnews.com/pictures/worst-movies-2021/

Rotten Tomatoes contributors. "100 Worst Movies of All Time". Rotten Tomatoes. https://editorial.rottentomatoes.com/guide/worst-movies-of-all-time/

Rotten Tomatoes contributors. "140 Essential '70s Movies". Rotten Tomatoes. https://editorial.rottentomatoes.com/guide/140-essential-70s-movies/

Rotten Tomatoes contributors. "140 Essential '80s Movies". Rotten Tomatoes. https://editorial.rottentomatoes.com/guide/140-essential-80s-movies/

Rotten Tomatoes contributors. "140 Essential '90s Movies". Rotten Tomatoes. https://editorial.rottentomatoes.com/guide/140-essential-90s-movies/

Rotten Tomatoes contributors. "140 Essential 2000s Movies". Rotten Tomatoes. https://editorial.rottentomatoes.com/guide/essential-2000s-movies/

Rum and Raspberries, IMDB contributors. "IMDB 366 Weird Movies FULL LIST - from 366weirdmovies.com". The Internet Movie Database. https://www.listchallenges.com/366-weird-movies-full-list

Scheider, Steven Jay, and Ian Haydn Smith. 1001 Movies You Must See Before You Die. Barron's Educational Series, Inc., 2015.

Tannenbaum, Emily, and Hanna Dickinson. "19 Serial Killer Movies You Will Enjoy Despite the Serious Trust Issues They'll Give You" Cosmopolitan. 12 Aug 2020: https://www.cosmopolitan.com/entertainment/movies/a28101043/serial-killer-movies/

The Editors of Cosmopolitan. "48 Christmas Movies That Will Make You Feel Like Human Tinsel". Cosmopolitan. 7 Dec. 2020: https://www.cosmopolitan.com/entertainment/movies/a17484/best-christmas-movies-ever/

TheFabulousThomasJ. IMDB Contributor. "All-Time Best Films MADE FOR TV". The Internet Movie Database. 30 Mar 2011: https://www.imdb.com/list/ls000757081/

Thomas, Jeremy. "The Top 10 Worst Movies of 2021 (So Far)". 411 Mania. 14 July 2021: https://411mania.com/movies/the-top-10-worst-movies-of-2021-so-far/

Thompson, Jeremy, Nathan Chase and Filmsite contributors. "Greatest Films by Year" Filmsite, Greatest Films. https://www.filmsite.org/greatestfilms-byyear.html

Thompson, Jeremy, Nathan Chase and Flickchart contributors. "The Top 100 Comedies of the 2000s". Flickchart. https://www.flickchart.com/Charts.aspx?genre=Comedy&decade=2000&perpage=100

Utz, Daniel and Benedikt Groß. Open Moji. https://openmoji.org/library/

Vaičiulaitytė, Giedrė and Damanjeet Sethi. "118 Fun Facts About Movies (Spoiler: Kate Winslet Is Especially Naughty)". Bored Panda. 26 Jun 2018: https://www.boredpanda.com/interesting-movie-facts/

Wikipedia contributors. "Academy Awards." Wikipedia, The Free Encyclopedia, 28 Dec. 2020. Web. 7 Jan 2021.

Wikipedia contributors. "Cinema of France." Wikipedia, The Free Encyclopedia, 27 Nov. 2020. Web. 7 Jan 2021.

Wikipedia contributors. "Golden Globe Awards." Wikipedia, The Free Encyclopedia. 6 Jan 2021. Web. 7 Jan 2021.

Wikipedia contributors. "Golden Raspberry Awards."Wikipedia, The Free Encyclopedia. 3 Jan. 2021. Web. 7 Jan 2021

Wikipedia contributors. "History of film." Wikipedia, The Free Encyclopedia. 22 Jan 2021. Web. 24 Jan 2021.

Wikipedia contributors. "List of Cinematic Firsts". Wikipedia, The Free Encyclopedia. Wikipedia, The Free Encyclopedia, 16 Jun. 2024. Web. 22 Jun. 2024.

Wikipedia contributors. "List of Criterion Collection releases." Wikipedia, The Free Encyclopedia. Wikipedia, The Free Encyclopedia, 5 Jan 2021. Web. 7 Jan 2021.

Wikipedia contributors. "List of films considered the best." Wikipedia, The Free Encyclopedia. 6 Jan. 2021. Web. 7 Jan 2021.

Wikipedia contributors. "List of years in film." Wikipedia, The Free Encyclopedia. Wikipedia, The Free Encyclopedia, 5 Jan 2021. Web. 7 Jan. 2021.

Wunderdunder, IMDB contributor. "History of Movie Firsts." The Internet Movie Database. 23 June 2011: https://www.imdb.com/list/ls000930391/

YA728, List Challenges contributor. "50 Weird Movies". List Challenges. https://www.listchallenges.com/50-weird-movies

Zilko Christian and Christian Blauvelt. "The 50 Best Movies of 2023, According to 158 Critics from Around the World". Indiewire. 6 Mar 2024: https://www.indiewire.com/gallery/50-best-movies-of-2023-critics-survey/

Zulekia B., Fandom contributor. "7 Best Anime Movies of 2018, Ranked." Fandom. 25 Dec 2018: https://www.fandom.com/articles/best-anime-movies-2018-ranked

Zulekia B., Fandom contributor. "The 7 Best Anime Movies of 2017". Fandom. 27 Dec 2017: https://www.fandom.com/articles/7-best-anime-movies-2017

Zulekia B., Fandom contributor. "The 15 Best Anime of 2016". Fandom. 18 Dec 2016: https://www.fandom.com/articles/15-best-anime-2016

Zulekia B., Fandom contributor. "The 15 Best Anime of 2017". Fandom. 19 Dec 2017: https://www.fandom.com/articles/15-best-anime-2017

<u>LIGHTS, CAMERA, CALL TO ACTION!</u>

Hello there! Tremendous thanks again for purchasing **"The Cinephile Catalogue!"** As Rick from "Casablanca" once said, "*I think this is the beginning of a beautiful friendship.*"

Please leave your review for "The Cinephile Catalogue," on Amazon, Google, Apple Books, Barnes and Noble or wherever you buy books! Your opinion matters and is always appreciated!

I read every single review, and your reviews will help cinephiles and movie lovers discover this book. Please hashtag **#TCC** & **#thecinephilecatalogue** on social and post about all the ways you use your TCC! My absolute gratitude to you all!

Keep seeing movies! Keep loving movies! And most importantly, support your local cinema and movie houses!

Peace and Love to You & Yours!

 **@thecinephilecatalogue**    **@TCCBook @CinemaNYC**